Reading this book alone is a [illegible] *dy for healthy relationships."* [illegible] ou love and work with, and en[illegible] t's transformational.

Share it with your spouse. Bring [illegible] with friends, coworkers, adult children, or extended relatives. Anywhere two or more people connect, this book will strengthen the bond.

And if you read it by yourself, don't underestimate your influence. One informed, self-aware person can shift the entire relational climate. When you understand the three silent relationship killers—and how they hide inside everyday stressors—you become a catalyst for change.

This book transforms you individually—but shared, it transforms communities.

Contents

Introduction: The Power of Attitude, Expectations, and Assumptions™ in Relationships

Relationships—whether with family, friends, romantic partners, coworkers, or within our communities—are the foundation of human life. Relationships influence every corner of our lives. They color our daily experiences, surround us with comfort and support, and anchor us in a sense of belonging—at work, in our personal lives, and throughout our communities. In professional settings, strong relationships spark collaboration and elevate productivity by helping us draw from the strengths and talents of those around us. In our personal relationships, they nurture trust, emotional stability, and shared growth. Within our communities, they foster unity, compassion, and a deeper commitment to collective well-being. When we choose to value and leverage the unique gifts others carry, we create space for our own strengths to rise, allowing each of us to contribute at our highest potential.. Yet, even the most cherished relationships can unravel in the face of unseen forces—forces we often fail to recognize until it's too late. Attitude, assumptions, and expectations—subtle but powerful influences—shape how we perceive and engage with others. They determine whether our friendships deepen or fade, whether our romantic relationships flourish or falter, and whether our professional connections lead to collaboration or conflict. For years, I pointed to the obvious friction points and believed they were the reason my relationships fell apart. But those things were only symptoms—stressors, not causes. The deeper truth is that the success or failure of any relationship begins with each individual in it, and with the patterns we carry into those connections.

Why This Phenomenon Applies to Every Person on the Planet: *The Universal Importance of Relationships Across Belief Systems*

No matter where a person is born, what language they speak, or which belief system shapes their worldview, one truth remains constant: human beings are wired for connection. Relationships are not optional—they are essential. Every major faith tradition, philosophical viewpoint, and cultural framework teaches some version of this idea, even though the language and rituals may differ. These teachings stretch across continents, history, and entire civilizations, all pointing to the same reality: people thrive when their relationships are healthy and crumble internally when they are not.

Christianity often emphasizes love, forgiveness, and service as cornerstones of spiritual life. These principles are rooted in the belief that relationships are sacred and that healing, reconciliation, and generosity strengthen communities and honor God.

Islam teaches kindness, patience, and compassion as essential virtues, reflecting the idea that relationships shape moral character and that treating others with dignity is an act of faith.

Judaism places strong value on respect, honesty, and mutual support within families and communities, viewing relationships as a reflection of covenant, responsibility, and shared identity.

Hinduism highlights compassion, duty, and spiritual growth, suggesting that fulfilling one's responsibilities toward others is a pathway to personal and spiritual harmony.

Buddhism underscores interconnectedness, compassion, and kindness. It teaches that suffering is lessened when we understand our connection to others and approach relationships with intentional care.

Indigenous belief systems across the world—whether in Africa, the Americas, Australia, or the Pacific—teach harmony, reciprocity, and balance. Relationships extend beyond people to include ancestors, land, animals, and the natural world, emphasizing deep interdependence.

Atheism and secular worldviews may not rely on spiritual doctrine, but they still recognize the importance of human connection, empathy, emotional intelligence, and personal growth. Secular psychology and sociology confirm that meaningful relationships directly influence mental health, identity, and life satisfaction.

Across all of these perspectives, a common thread emerges: Healthy relationships are central to emotional stability, personal development, ultimate life satisfaction, and communal strength.
They determine how people heal, how they work, how they raise families, and how they build societies. They shape cultures, influence ethics, define values, and guide how individuals see themselves in relation to the world.

Even though the philosophies differ, the message is the same across every belief system and every society on earth:

We are better, stronger, healthier, and more fulfilled when we are in connection with other people.

But if relationships are so vital, what happens when these invisible forces go unchecked? How does a close friendship erode into resentment? Why do once-promising romantic partnerships end in heartbreak? What makes a respected leader—once admired for their vision and competence—become isolated or even removed from their position? In the workplace, misunderstandings rooted in unspoken assumptions can create toxic environments. In romantic relationships, unmet expectations can breed disappointment and distance. In friendships, unchecked attitudes can lead to quiet disconnection.

This book will uncover how attitude, expectations, and assumptions™ shape every type of relationship in our lives—whether personal, professional, or romantic. We will explore the ways these forces can create cracks in even the strongest foundations, but also how awareness and intentionality can repair and strengthen our connections. By recognizing and addressing these hidden influences, we can cultivate deeper trust, greater understanding, and more fulfilling relationships in every area of life.

But before we can fully understand how attitude, assumptions, and expectations shape our relationships, we must first understand why they exist at all. These patterns are not random. They are not character flaws, emotional weaknesses, or personality quirks. They are ***deeply rooted psychological responses*** — survival strategies wired into the human brain. Long before we learn communication skills or emotional intelligence, our nervous system is already scanning for safety, certainty, and belonging. To truly transform our relationships and leadership impact, we must first understand the psychology beneath the surf

Chapter 1: The Power of Attitude, Expectations, and Assumptions in Relationships

Relationships are the cornerstone of human connection. And while we often experience their challenges on the surface — through conflict, disappointment, misunderstanding, and emotional distance — what is truly shaping those moments is happening beneath the surface. Whether in the workplace, at home, or in our friendships, our attitudes, assumptions, and expectations quietly guide how we interpret, respond, and connect.

In every aspect of connection, relationships provide us with support, companionship, and a sense of belonging. Yet, despite their importance, even the strongest relationships can face challenges when invisible forces—attitudes, expectations, and assumptions—creep in. These three elements shape how we perceive and interact with others, influencing everything from our communication styles to our behavior and responses. If left unchecked, they can lead to misunderstandings, resentment, and conflict, eroding the very foundation of trust and respect upon which healthy relationships are built. Let's examine how these forces impact our connections—and how, when you summon the courage and commitment to grow, you can gain the power to reshape every relationship you touch, both now and moving forward.

The Attitude Shift: *The Energy We Bring*

One of my favorite authors, Joyce Meyer, captures the essence of attitude brilliantly. She says our attitude is simply our thoughts and emotions turned inside out. You don't have to say a word—your attitude shows all on its own. What's powerful is that, at the end of the day, awareness gives us the ability to influence it. I used to define attitude as the way we position or posture ourselves toward a person, idea, situation, or concept. But Joyce's perspective really hits home for me!

Have you ever heard the saying, "It's all about your attitude"? Well, in relationships, attitude is EVERYTHING. Our outlook—whether positive, negative, or neutral—shapes how we interpret actions, words, and intentions. A positive attitude towards others can create harmony, build trust, and foster growth. On the flip side, a negative or cynical attitude can breed defensiveness, hurt feelings, and walls that separate us from others.

Imagine you're having a conversation with a friend, but you're already frustrated from a long day. If your attitude is closed off or defensive, your friend's words—no matter how innocent—may seem like an attack. But if your attitude is open and patient, you'll likely find more understanding and connection.

Attitude isn't just how we feel—it's a lens that colors everything. The key to cultivating better relationships? Choose your attitude wisely, knowing that it can either build bridges or burn them.

As you move through this book, you'll develop the ability to notice when your attitude drifts off course. That recognition is a remarkable strength, because awareness hands you the choice—and the responsibility—to adjust it.

Expectations: *The Silent Architects of Our Relationships*

Expectations are like the unwritten rules of engagement in any relationship. They define how we think people should behave and how we expect them to meet our needs. Expectations are cognitive forecasts that shape emotional weather; unmet, they storm our peace. But the tricky part? We often don't communicate these expectations, leaving others unaware of what we need, or worse, pressuring them to meet standards they can't fulfill. Unintentionally, even unconsciously, we tend to expect friends to always be available to listen, no matter what's going on in their own lives. At first, they may happily oblige, but over time, this might feel like a burden. When they can't meet that need, frustration builds—on both sides. This leads to resentment, distance, and ultimately, dissatisfaction.

But not all expectations are harmful. When expectations are realistic and communicated openly, they can help strengthen the bond between two people. If you expect your friends to treat you with kindness, and they do, that creates a foundation of trust. If you expect honesty and they're truthful with you, that solidifies respect. The challenge is ensuring your expectations are clear, manageable, and, most importantly, mutual. While unspoken and unrealistic expectations harm personal relationships, their impact in professional and community spaces can be even more destructive. They can destabilize a business, create toxic team dynamics, and turn groups with shared missions into places marked by conflict and hostility.

Assumptions: *The Silent Saboteurs*

Assumptions are those sneaky thoughts we have about what others think, feel, or intend—without actually asking. We often assume people know how we feel, or we may assume they understand what we need without saying a word. But the truth is, assumptions are rarely accurate. And the more we rely on them, the more we misunderstand each other.

Let's say your friend doesn't respond to your text immediately. You might assume they're upset with you, or that they don't care. But in reality, they may just be busy or dealing with their own challenges. Instead of assuming, taking the time to ask and clarify can avoid unnecessary tension and keep the relationship strong.

Assumptions not only cause misunderstandings but also prevent growth. They keep us stuck in old patterns, afraid to ask the difficult questions or have the uncomfortable conversations that could lead to deeper understanding.

Whereas attitudes and expectations can outwardly affect the people around us, assumptions do something far more damaging—they turn inward and quietly eat away at your soul. They keep your mind in a cycle of turmoil, fueled by thoughts that are usually untrue. Assumptions can isolate you, placing you on an emotional island where every worry feels heavier and every doubt feels louder. Over time, they erode your peace, drain your emotional health, and distance you from the very connections you need most.

Conclusion: The Power of Healthy Relationships

Across all cultures, religions, and belief systems, one truth remains constant: human relationships are fundamental to our well-being. Whether through love, respect, service, or compassion, every tradition recognizes the deep need for connection. Friendships, romantic relationships, workplace dynamics, and community ties all shape our lives, providing support, purpose, and fulfillment. However, despite this universal truth, relationships are often strained or broken—not by a lack of importance, but by unseen forces that creep in unnoticed.

So, if relationships are essential to a meaningful life, what threatens them? What causes once-strong bonds to unravel? The answer lies in the very forces that shape our interactions: attitude, expectations, and assumptions. When left unchecked, they can distort perceptions, fuel misunderstandings, and ultimately destroy the very connections we rely on.

Read this true example of how those silent destroyers came dangerously close to derailing one of the most defining moments of my career.

Storytime – Real Life Examples

In 2013, I moved to the Middle East to work in education reform—7,637 miles from home. I left behind a school where I had worked hard to unite a divided team and was now stepping into an entirely new environment: a country with different beliefs, a different language, and a culture shaped by Islam. My role was to prepare a large school for global accreditation.

The United Arab Emirates is a young nation—established around 1972—rooted in Islamic values that deserved deep respect. As I introduced Western educational methods, I had to balance progress with cultural sensitivity. My first few weeks were difficult, not because of lack of skill, but because of assumptions, expectations, and attitudes—on both sides.

The staff assumed I was there to replace local leaders, so they met me with resistance. I remember walking down the hall to meet the team and watching the leader spot me and turn around to avoid the introduction. Their attitude toward an outsider telling them what to do was defensive and closed off. They ignored my presence and continued working as before—even though their methods no longer fit their growing reality.

Their school had expanded from several small neighborhood sites serving fewer than 100 students each to a single large school serving over 800. That leap required new structure and systems, but change felt threatening.

My own expectations added tension. I expected the staff and leadership to follow my lead simply because I had seventeen years of leadership experience. I assumed that once they saw my dedication, trust would come naturally and collaboration would follow. Instead, those expectations got me nowhere. They widened the divide and intensified the fear some held—that the Westerners were coming to replace the local educators. As a result, progress was slow and filled with resistance.

Realizing this, I shifted my approach. I looked for an area where I could meet them in their struggle—somewhere new to them but familiar to me. That critical issue turned out to be the student–teacher master schedule, the system that determined which teachers taught which students, which classrooms were assigned, and how to feed 800 children in just 90 minutes. Because it was unfamiliar to them, it had become complete chaos: multiple teachers assigned to the same classroom, ninety displaced students—three entire classes without teachers—and lunch happening for four hundred students with no supervision structure in place.

Eventually, I was asked to fix the schedule, one of the areas where I naturally excelled. I could tell they wanted to succeed without relying on me, and that mattered. So I adjusted my attitude and released every expectation I had placed on them. I chose to view the situation through their eyes and respond with empathy instead of pride. The truth was simple: I needed them, and they needed me. Once we reshaped our attitudes, examined our assumptions, and released our expectations, we found our rhythm—and from that unity, we moved confidently toward global accreditation.

The Courage to Keep Reading

As we prepare to step into Chapter 2 and explore the deeper psychological forces that quietly shape our reactions, patterns, and behaviors, pause for just a moment.

What is rising in you right now? What thoughts are surfacing?

By now, you've seen that these silent destroyers—attitude, assumptions, and expectations—reach into every corner of our relational lives. They influence how we show up, how we interpret others, and how tension takes root long before words are ever exchanged. This isn't just about identifying problems; it's about understanding how the patterns within us shape the connections we build everywhere we go.

Before you turn the page, take inventory of what's stirring inside you. Is there a relationship—past or present—that suddenly feels clearer? Is there a moment you now recognize as the turning point? Or maybe you feel the urge to close the book because honest reflection can feel unsettling.

If so, don't stop here. Lean in. Be courageous. Growth requires truth, and truth requires the willingness to look inward. As you continue reading, you will gain the awareness, the language, and the clarity to recognize the subtle forces that have shaped your relationships—and the tools to transform them. The journey ahead will challenge you, but it will also strengthen you. Stay with it. Your breakthrough is waiting.

Chapter 2: The Psychology Beneath the Surface: Why We Respond the Way We Do

Human behavior is not random. Our reactions, emotional patterns, and relational responses are shaped long before we consciously choose how to act. Beneath every tone of voice, emotional surge, defensive posture, or quiet withdrawal lies a powerful biological system designed for one primary purpose: survival.

Neuroscience and trauma psychology confirm that long before we learn communication skills, emotional intelligence, leadership strategies, or relational tools, our brains are already scanning our environment for safety, certainty, and belonging. Neuroscientist Dr. Stephen Porges describes this unconscious process as neuroception — the nervous system's constant evaluation of safety and threat — occurring largely outside our conscious awareness (Porges, 2011). In every interaction, our nervous system is silently asking: Am I safe? Am I seen? Do I belong? When safety is perceived, connection and growth become possible. But when threat is detected — whether physical, emotional, social, or relational — the nervous system immediately shifts into protection mode.

Psychologist and emotional intelligence researcher Dr. Daniel Goleman explains that during these moments, the brain's survival centers can override rational thinking in what he famously calls an emotional hijack (Goleman, 1995). Logic narrows. Emotional regulation tightens.

And behavior becomes driven more by instinct than by intention.

Instead of responding thoughtfully, we react reflexively — often in ways we later regret. Our tone sharpens. Our patience thins. Our defenses rise. And our capacity for empathy temporarily fades.

Trauma researcher Dr. Bruce Perry further explains that when the brain perceives threat, it shifts control away from higher reasoning centers and toward survival-oriented neural systems, prioritizing protection over reflection (Perry, 2009; Perry & Szalavitz, 2017). In these moments, the brain is not asking, What is the wisest response? but rather, What will keep me safe right now? This neurological shift helps explain why even emotionally intelligent, highly capable leaders and relationally aware individuals can find themselves reacting defensively, withdrawing, controlling situations, or emotionally shutting down.

Adding another layer of insight, psychiatrist and trauma expert Dr. Bessel van der Kolk reveals that the body itself stores emotional memory, meaning that past experiences of pain, rejection, abandonment, or fear can shape present reactions without conscious awareness (van der Kolk, 2014). Long after a threat has passed, the nervous system can continue to respond as though danger remains. This is why a simple tone of voice, facial expression, silence, or perceived slight can trigger reactions that feel disproportionate to the moment — the body is remembering, even when the mind does not.

Together, these findings reveal a profound truth: our attitudes, assumptions, and expectations are not merely habits or personality traits. They are deeply rooted psychological responses — automatic survival strategies designed to protect us from pain, rejection, uncertainty, and loss. Attitude becomes our emotional armor. Assumptions become our mental threat scanners. Expectations become our attempt to control uncertainty. When we understand this, we stop judging our reactions and start decoding them. And it is in that decoding that true transformation begins.

The AAE™ Survival Cascade: *How the Brain Translates Threat into Behavior*

Once the nervous system detects threat, it does not respond randomly. It follows a predictable sequence — one that quietly shapes how we think, feel, and behave in relationships and leadership spaces. This is where attitude, assumptions, and expectations come into play.

Rather than appearing as isolated habits, these three forces operate together as a psychological survival cascade — a process through which the brain translates perceived threat into emotional posture, mental narrative, and behavioral control.

In simple terms:

Threat → Attitude → Assumptions → Expectations → Behavior → Culture

This sequence explains why the same patterns repeat across different relationships, workplaces, and seasons of life. It also explains why awareness alone often isn't enough to create lasting change. Until we understand how the nervous system organizes our responses, we remain vulnerable to reacting automatically rather than responding intentionally.

Let's take a closer look at how each part of this cascade functions.

Attitude: *Our Emotional Armor*

Attitude is the first line of psychological defense. It is the emotional posture we adopt the moment our nervous system senses uncertainty, vulnerability, or threat.

Before words are spoken.
Before logic engages.
Before behavior is chosen.

We emotionally armor up.

Attitude becomes our emotional shield — protecting us from rejection, embarrassment, disappointment, failure, judgment, or loss of control. This armor can show up in many forms: defensiveness, emotional withdrawal, control, hyper-professionalism, sarcasm, rigidity, people-pleasing, or emotional detachment.

In leadership and relational spaces, this often looks like:

- Walking into conversations already guarded
- Preparing to defend rather than understand
- Controlling outcomes instead of trusting process
- Withholding vulnerability to avoid exposure

This is not weakness. It is biology.

When safety feels uncertain, the nervous system prioritizes protection. Attitude becomes the body's emotional response to perceived risk.

But armor, while protective, comes at a cost.

What shields us from pain can also block connection.
What guards us from rejection can also restrict intimacy.
What protects our vulnerability can also limit trust.

Leadership and relational maturity require learning when armor is necessary — and when awareness, openness, and emotional regulation must take its place.

Assumptions: *The Brain's Threat Interpretation System*

Once attitude is activated, the brain immediately begins interpreting the environment in ways that restore certainty and predictability. This is where assumptions emerge.

Assumptions function as mental shortcuts — rapid interpretations that help us make sense of ambiguity, silence, tone, and behavior. They answer questions like:

- What does this mean?
- What are they thinking?
- What is about to happen?
- Am I safe here?

Because the brain craves certainty, it often fills in missing information with stories drawn from past experiences, emotional memory, trauma, cultural conditioning, and identity narratives. These stories feel real — even when they are incomplete or inaccurate.

This is why:

We don't experience reality. We experience the story we tell ourselves about reality.

Assumptions can protect us — but they can also imprison us.

They can create meaning where none was intended.
They can fuel conflict where none existed.
They can generate fear in moments of neutrality.

And because assumptions often operate beneath conscious awareness, they quietly shape emotional response, tone, and relational posture long before we realize what is happening.

Expectations: *The Brain's Control Strategy*

When threat feels ongoing, the nervous system seeks **predictability**. This is where expectations emerge.

Expectations function as **psychological contracts** — internal rules about how people *should* behave, how relationships *should* function, and how leadership *should* unfold. They give the brain a sense of control, structure, and emotional safety.

We expect:

- People to respond in certain ways
- Relationships to meet unspoken needs
- Leaders to behave according to our internal standards
- Ourselves to perform flawlessly

When expectations are met, the nervous system relaxes. When they are violated, the nervous system alarms.

Disappointment, resentment, frustration, withdrawal, and emotional shutdown often follow — not because the situation was catastrophic, but because the brain experiences **loss of control and loss of predictability** as threat.

This is why unmet expectations can feel so emotionally intense — and why unspoken expectations are among the most destructive forces in relationships and leadership culture.

The AAE™ Psychological Cascade in Action

Together, attitude, assumptions, and expectations form a **self-reinforcing survival loop.**

When attitude becomes defensive →
assumptions become negative →
expectations become rigid →
behavior becomes reactive →
culture becomes tense.

But when attitude is regulated →
assumptions soften →
expectations clarify →
behavior becomes intentional →
culture becomes safe.

This is the **core psychological insight** of the AAE™ Framework.

Change does not begin with behavior.
It begins with **nervous system awareness**.

When we learn to recognize the moment our attitude armors, our assumptions distort, and our expectations tighten, we gain access to something powerful: **choice.**

And choice is the birthplace of transformation.

From Survival to Self-Awareness

The goal of growth is not to eliminate survival responses. They are essential. They have protected us. They have preserved us. They have helped us endure.

The goal is to **become aware of them.**

Awareness interrupts autopilot.
Awareness creates space.
Awareness restores agency.

When leaders learn to regulate their nervous systems, they do more than change their own experience — they reshape the emotional climate of entire organizations.

Because leadership is not just decision-making.
Leadership is emotional regulation in motion.

Your internal state becomes organizational culture.

And this is where AAE™ becomes transformational — not just informational.

From Awareness to Impact: How Survival Patterns Become Relationship Stressors

Understanding the psychology beneath our reactions changes everything — but insight alone does not remove the pressures that test our relationships every day. Life still brings conflict. People still disappoint us. Stress still weighs heavy. Trauma still echoes. And leadership still demands more than we often feel prepared to give.

This is where the internal becomes external.

When attitude armors, assumptions distort, and expectations tighten, these survival responses begin to show up in visible ways. They leak into our tone. They shape our words. They influence our decisions. They quietly reshape the emotional climate of our homes, friendships, workplaces, and communities.

Over time, these internal patterns create **relational stressors** — the friction points we experience as communication breakdowns, unresolved conflict, emotional distance, trust erosion, burnout, jealousy, insecurity, and disconnection. These stressors are not random. They are the surface expression of deeper psychological processes operating beneath awareness.

In other words:

> *Stressors are not the cause of relational breakdown — they are the symptoms.*

If we want lasting change, we must learn to recognize what these symptoms look like in real life. We must understand how survival responses translate into everyday relational challenges — and how small, seemingly insignificant moments accumulate into emotional distance, resentment, and fracture.

This brings us to the next critical question:

If human beings are biologically wired for connection, what keeps tearing our relationships apart?

Chapter 3: What Destroys This Universal Need for Relationships?

If relationships are so fundamental to a healthy, successful life, **what on earth keeps tearing them apart?**

How does a couple — once full of dreams, shared playlists, vision boards, and matching coffee mugs — end up barely speaking, tiptoeing around each other in tense silence?

How does a deep friendship built on laughter, secrets, and late-night vent sessions slowly unravel into emotional distance and awkward small talk?

How does a visionary leader — once praised for brilliance, innovation, and influence — suddenly find themselves unemployed, disconnected from their network, and binge-watching motivational TED Talks alone, wondering what went wrong?

We've already established that human beings are biologically wired for connection. Our relationships provide love, support, meaning, and that all-important sense of belonging. They are not optional — they are essential. In fact, healthy relationships are directly linked to emotional well-being, professional success, physical health, and overall life satisfaction.

And yet, they are also remarkably fragile.

Sometimes, all it takes is **a single misstep. A misunderstood comment. An unspoken expectation. A tone that lands wrong.** In a matter of moments, connection can begin to fracture.

Why is that?

Because relationships don't exist in a vacuum. They live under constant pressure from emotional, social, cultural, professional, and psychological forces — some obvious, others far more subtle. Some walk through the front door. Others slip in quietly, like emotional ninjas, shaping our reactions before we even realize they've arrived.

In this chapter, we will explore the most common **relationship stressors** — the visible points of friction that show up as communication breakdowns, unresolved conflict, emotional withdrawal, jealousy, insecurity, burnout, and disconnection. Some of these will sound familiar (cue the collective eye-roll for "communication problems"), but don't be fooled. These stressors are not the true culprits.

Think of them as **smoke — the visible signal of a deeper fire.**

Beneath every stressor lies one of three powerful psychological forces: **attitude, assumptions, or expectations.**

These are the real relationship wrecking balls.

Diving Into the Stressors

3A. Lack of Communication

Communication is often described as the foundation of every healthy relationship. And it's true — until that foundation starts cracking. What happens when people stop talking? Or when they only say what's easy instead of what's honest? When listening becomes nothing more than waiting for your turn to speak?

The result is predictable: confusion. Frustration. Misunderstandings that snowball into full-blown conflict. Over time, silence grows louder than words, and the connection that once felt effortless begins to fade.

How on earth did you find yourselves here?

But communication isn't the root of the problem.

Somewhere along the way, something happened — an incident, a misunderstanding, unaddressed hurt feelings, a shift in emotional energy — and one, but most likely both of you, responded with one or more of the three silent relationship destroyers. Face it, we tend to match each other's energy unless we intentionally choose not to. If your communication issues are relatively new, I'm actually excited for you, because you can probably trace the moment the breakdown began.

People don't just stop communicating out of nowhere.

We pull back when we've made assumptions.
We withdraw when our needs go unmet.
We shut down when an attitude forms that pushes us further apart instead of pulling us together.

Can you identify the moment in a relationship that is suffering, where communication first became strained? More often than not, lack of communication begins with assumptions — but attitudes and expectations are always close behind, ready to make things worse.

Lack of Communication & Assumptions: *Misunderstanding's Favorite Sidekick*

Let's be honest — most communication breakdowns begin with one simple thing: assuming.

We assume our partner can read our mind.
We assume our friend's silence is personal.
We assume our colleague understood the plan we never clearly explained.

And as mentioned earlier, assumptions don't just damage relationships — they can also wreak havoc on your mental health.

In short, we assume people "just know."

Spoiler: they don't.

- **Personal relationships:** "They should just know I need help." (Did you say that out loud? No?)
- **Friendships:** "She didn't call me back — she must be over me." (Or maybe she's stuck in traffic with a dead phone.)
- **Workplace dynamics:** "Everyone knows what I meant." (Except they don't. And now the presentation is forty-five empty slides and a vague title.)

In diverse environments — schools buzzing with conflict, workplaces balancing pressure, cross-cultural teams navigating worlds within a single room, and even inside our own homes — assumptions don't just grow. They stalk the space like shadows. One unspoken thought becomes two, then ten, then an entire story no one ever actually said aloud.

With different communication styles, clashing values, and unspoken expectations swirling in the air, clarity becomes the difference between harmony and disaster. But instead of reaching for it, everyone retreats. Eyes down. Lips sealed. Minds racing. Everyone trapped in their own internal dialogue, and no one brave enough to break the silence.

Then it happens.

Mistakes land like landmines. Feelings get crushed. Boundaries are crossed. Trust fractures.

In families, people tiptoe.
In friendships, distance grows.
In relationships, tension thickens.
In workplaces, pressure becomes suffocating.

Yet still — silence.

Everyone assumes: They should've known. They should've understood. They should've done better.

The moment passes on the surface, but underneath, resentment simmers. Then another moment hits — eerily similar — and the cycle tightens.

When communication finally erupts, it's not a calm conversation. It's a storm. Words fly. Voices rise. Tears fall. Doors slam. Phones go unanswered. People shut down, walk out, emotionally disappear, or quietly disengage.

And afterward, avoidance becomes the default.

People whisper to themselves that communication has failed.

But communication didn't fail. Your assumptions did.

Lack of Communication & Expectations: *The Unspoken Rulebook*

Unspoken expectations are like invisible contracts we silently expect others to sign and obey. We want loved ones to check in, friends to show up, and supervisors to recognize our effort — yet we rarely state these expectations clearly.

When people don't live up to what they never knew we wanted, resentment builds. And resentment never plays fair.

Unlike assumptions, which often keep us trapped in our own heads, unmet expectations tend to come out as direct attacks. We lash out over what didn't happen, what wasn't said, or what wasn't done "the right way," even though those standards were never spoken aloud.

In these moments, we say, "communication is broken," when in reality, communication was never fully established.

So pause and reflect:

What exactly is bothering you?
Did you actually communicate the expectation that wasn't met?
Was the other person even able to meet it, given everything they were carrying?

Before confronting someone about what they didn't do, make sure you've done your part — by clearly expressing what you needed.

Lack of Communication & Attitude: *When Mindset Gets in the Way*

Sometimes, our attitude toward communication becomes the real barrier. Maybe we avoid conflict. Maybe vulnerability feels unbearable. Maybe we've convinced ourselves, It won't matter anyway.

Whatever the reason, we adopt an attitude that tells us silence is safer than honesty.

But here's the truth: **avoidance doesn't protect relationships — it erodes them.**

Unspoken issues don't resolve themselves. They grow roots. They spread. They deepen.

Often, communication feels frightening because conflict awakens old wounds or unresolved trauma. That is understandable. But growth requires courage. Healing requires honesty. Healthy relationships demand that we examine our attitude toward communication itself.

The relationship didn't fall apart because communication failed.

It fell apart because fear silenced communication before it ever had a chance.

Breaking the Cycle

If assumptions, expectations, and attitude fuel the breakdown of communication, how do we stop the cycle?

It starts with awareness.

Catch yourself when you're assuming instead of asking.
Replace expectations with honest conversations.
Shift your attitude from *Why bother?* to *This matters.*

Clarity creates connection. And clear, compassionate communication is always worth the effort.

Reflection Activity

Let's get personal for a moment.

Think about your relationships — romantic, platonic, and professional. Ask yourself:

- Do I avoid difficult conversations? Why?
- Do I assume others should "just know" how I feel?
- Have I formed a negative attitude before giving the conversation a chance?
- Do I hold people to expectations they don't even know exist?

Identifying your communication pattern is the first step toward changing it.

Now, think of a recent miscommunication or conflict. Write it down. Then ask yourself: **Was the breakdown rooted in attitude, assumption, or expectation?**

Identifying the pattern you have when it comes to communication is your first step to changing it. Pay attention next time it shows up—and try something different. Because better communication doesn't just repair relationships. It strengthens them from the inside out.

Activity: Now, think of a recent miscommunication or conflict. Write it down. Then ask yourself: was the breakdown rooted in attitude, assumption, or expectation?

3B. Dishonesty or Deception

Trust is the cornerstone of every meaningful relationship—whether with a partner, a friend, or a colleague. When trust is damaged, the impact can feel devastating. Acts such as lying, withholding information, manipulating the truth, or using deception for personal gain create fractures that are often difficult—and sometimes impossible—to repair. Betrayal doesn't just break the moment; it erodes the entire foundation of the relationship, leaving behind confusion, hurt, and emotional distance.

What's often hardest to understand is that the real destroyer isn't always the dishonesty itself. *Dishonesty is the symptom.* It is something we engage in when we are trying to hide, avoid, manipulate, or protect ourselves. So, the next time someone close to you is dishonest—or you find yourself tempted to stretch the truth—pause and ask:

What am I trying to avoid?
What am I trying to gain?
What fear or wound am I protecting?

For many people, repeated dishonesty grows from a deeply rooted **attitude of self-protection.** This mindset is often tied to early experiences—especially childhood trauma—where telling the truth felt dangerous, risky, or met with harsh consequences. In those environments, deception becomes less of a choice and more of a survival instinct.

But dishonesty can also stem from an attitude of entitlement or control—using lies to manipulate situations, manage perceptions, or gain advantage. Whether driven by fear or self-gain, the underlying issue remains the same:

Attitude shapes behavior long before the lie is ever spoken.

Below are the deeper dynamics that reveal how attitude, expectations, and assumptions quietly fuel deception.

Dishonesty or Deception & Attitude: *The Core of Deception*

At its root, dishonesty stems from a person's attitude toward truth, trust, and integrity. Our mindset determines whether honesty feels safe—or threatening.

Self-preservation: When someone fears conflict or consequences, their attitude may lead them to lie or withhold information to avoid discomfort.

Manipulation: When someone views relationships as transactional, deception becomes a tool to gain power, control, or advantage.

Insecurity: When someone doubts their worth, they may alter the truth to appear more desirable, competent, or acceptable.

A person's underlying attitude toward honesty dictates whether deception becomes a coping mechanism—or a line they refuse to cross.

Dishonesty or Deception & Expectations: *Pressure to Perform, Pressure to Deceive*

Unrealistic or rigid expectations often create environments where dishonesty feels necessary.

In romantic relationships: A partner may hide feelings, past experiences, or desires to meet an idealized version of love.

In friendships: Someone may pretend to be okay because they feel pressure to remain "the strong one."

In professional spaces: Employees may exaggerate accomplishments or hide mistakes to meet unattainable performance standards.

When people believe they must live up to impossible expectations, deception often feels safer than disappointment.

Dishonesty or Deception & Assumptions

Misguided Justifications for Lying

Dishonesty is frequently fueled by assumptions about how truth will be received:

- *If I tell the truth, they won't understand.*
- *They'll leave me if they find out.*
- *Everyone else does it, so it must be okay.*

These narratives may feel protective, but they quietly erode trust. When we assume the worst outcome, we often justify deception—only to create the very disconnection we feared.

Breaking the Cycle

Since dishonesty is shaped by our attitudes, expectations, and assumptions, overcoming it requires deep self-awareness and courageous honesty.

The first step is challenging the belief that deception is necessary for survival, acceptance, or success. When we set realistic expectations with others, we remove much of the pressure that pushes us toward hiding the truth. And when we question our assumptions about how people will respond, we often discover that honesty brings relief, not rejection.

As you grow in truthfulness, don't be afraid to gently confront deception in people you love. Sometimes the most healing question you can ask is:

"Did you say that to protect yourself?" or "You don't have to inflate the truth to be accepted—we already accept you."

These conversations require courage.

But breaking a cycle of deception—whether in yourself or someone close to you—is work worth doing. It restores trust, rebuilds connection, and creates space for real healing.

Because while deception slowly erodes relationships, honesty—especially when it feels uncomfortable—creates the stability, clarity, and intimacy that lasting relationships depend on.

Reflection Activity

Let's get honest for a moment.

This exercise may feel uncomfortable because most of us justify our "little white lies." But growth begins with truth—and yes, *all of us have been dishonest at some point.* If you know someone who never has, please introduce me. I would genuinely love to meet them.

If you've read my first book, *I Wish Someone Would Have Told Me That!*, you know that my childhood and young adulthood were filled with challenges. The first lie I remember telling was about my age. I wanted a job before I was legally old enough, so I claimed to be sixteen when I was actually fourteen. That single deception placed me in an environment where I met the father of my first child. A relationship built on dishonesty eventually led to becoming a teenage mother.

That wasn't the only time I stretched the truth. Like many of us, I altered details, omitted facts, and reshaped narratives to survive circumstances I didn't yet know how to face. But healing taught me something invaluable:

Truth always works in our favor.

Activity:
Write down a time when you chose dishonesty to get what you wanted or avoid what you feared. Then release the guilt. Freedom begins when truth replaces shame.

Final Reflection:
The relationship with my daughter's father didn't last—and deception certainly contributed. But more than the lies themselves, it was my *attitude toward truth* that caused the greatest damage. Deep down, I believed control would protect me. But God taught me something far greater:
Truth builds what fear destroys.

Now it's your turn.

Write it down.
Release the burden.
And choose honesty.

Ch 3C. Unresolved Conflict:

Conflict is **good.** It is how we grow. Conflict is not a sign that something is broken—it is evidence that two people, or even two teams, care enough to show up with their full selves. Conflict is inevitable in any relationship, whether at home or in the workplace. It's not a matter of *if* it happens, but **how we respond when it does** that ultimately defines the strength of the bond, the health of the culture, and the level of trust within the relationship or team.

From a psychological perspective, conflict activates our nervous system. When tension rises, our bodies begin scanning for threat, safety, and control. If that system becomes overwhelmed, emotional regulation decreases, defensiveness increases, and productive dialogue quickly shuts down. When conflict is ignored, avoided, or mishandled, it begins to fester. What could have been a simple misunderstanding grows into resentment, silence, tension, disengagement, and emotional distance. Unresolved conflict drains emotional energy, builds invisible walls, and slowly erodes connection.

Unresolved conflict is most closely tied to **attitude**, and attitude remains the primary underlying destroyer during moments of stress, disagreement, and relational strain. Expectations and assumptions play powerful supporting roles, but **attitude determines whether we move toward resolution or retreat into protection.** Together, these three forces—attitude, expectations, and assumptions—either calm the nervous system or activate it, fueling emotional escalation or fostering emotional safety.

Conflict exposes what we expect from others, the stories we tell ourselves about their intentions, and the emotional posture we bring into difficult conversations. And this is precisely where growth occurs.

We grow through conflict when we stop interpreting it as an attack and begin viewing it as information—information about our needs, boundaries, fears, emotional triggers, and the health of the relationship or organizational culture. Instead of reacting defensively or withdrawing emotionally, conflict invites us to pause, regulate, and ask: *What is this moment teaching me about myself?*

Growth happens when we listen without rehearsing our rebuttal, when we speak truth without hostility, and when we remain emotionally present rather than shutting down or emotionally disconnecting.

In both personal and professional relationships, working through conflict with honesty and courage strengthens trust. It demonstrates that the relationship is resilient—that it can withstand tension, vulnerability, and truth. In the workplace, this creates psychological safety, deeper collaboration, healthier communication patterns, and stronger performance because emotional energy is no longer wasted navigating unspoken tension.

When both sides commit to engaging rather than avoiding, conflict becomes a **turning point.** It replaces assumptions with clarity, recalibrates expectations, repairs trust, and deepens emotional connection. Most importantly, we grow in conflict when we transform our patterns instead of repeating them. Every conflict becomes an opportunity to practice emotional regulation, communicate intentionally, establish healthy boundaries, and release habits that no longer serve us.

Conflict is not the enemy—**avoidance is.**

And avoidance is rooted in **attitude.**

What makes you shrink away from conflict?

When we approach conflict with emotional regulation, curiosity, and a healthier attitude, it becomes one of the most powerful tools for growth, healing, productivity, and relational strength—in every area of life.

Unresolved Conflict & Attitude: *Avoidance vs. Engagement*

Our approach to conflict always begins with **attitude.** Before a word is spoken, the emotional posture we carry determines how our nervous system responds. If we view confrontation as dangerous, threatening, or overwhelming, our nervous system shifts into protection mode—leading us to avoid, freeze, or shut down. Silence feels safer than vulnerability. But silence does not dissolve problems; it buries them alive, where they quietly grow.

On the other hand, if we interpret disagreement as a personal attack, our nervous system moves into defense. Every correction feels like criticism. Every conversation becomes a battlefield. Walls rise, empathy collapses, and productive dialogue disappears.

For others, conflict triggers a need for control. Pride becomes armor. Apologizing feels like weakness. Vulnerability feels unsafe. Yet unresolved conflict does not fade with time—it slowly erodes trust, emotional safety, and intimacy.

Ultimately, how we **think about conflict** determines whether we face it with courage or retreat in fear. And while problems never disappear on their own, relationships absolutely can. Choosing a regulated, growth-centered attitude toward conflict is choosing the relationship itself.

Unresolved Conflict & Expectations: *The Silent Saboteurs*

Unresolved conflict is often fueled by unspoken or unrealistic expectations—those invisible rules about how someone *should* behave, respond, or intuitively "just know."

In romantic relationships, one partner may expect emotional understanding without expressing emotional needs. In friendships, someone may expect constant availability. In professional spaces, employees may expect recognition or validation that is never clearly communicated. When these expectations go unmet, disappointment quietly transforms into resentment.

Because expectations remain unspoken, they become **silent saboteurs**, creating pressure, emotional distance, and misinterpretation. Instead of generating connection, they generate confusion. Instead of fostering trust, they deepen frustration.

Unresolved Conflict & Assumptions: *Fuel for the Fire*

Assumptions intensify unresolved conflict by shaping the internal stories we create about others' motives, thoughts, and intentions.

They don't care.
If I bring it up, it will only make things worse.
They should already know why I'm upset.

These narratives feel protective, but they cloud reality. When we assume instead of ask, communication collapses before it begins. Conflict thrives in that silence—fueled not by facts, but by the stories our nervous system constructs to maintain emotional safety.

Breaking the Cycle

Breaking the cycle of unresolved conflict begins with the courage to confront what you've been avoiding. Cycles don't break accidentally—they break when someone chooses to respond differently.

This requires confronting your attitude first: the fear, pride, assumptions, and expectations that have kept you silent or reactive. It means shifting from avoidance to emotional regulation, from defensiveness to curiosity, from fear to courage.

Instead of running from conflict, you name it.
Instead of assuming, you ask.
Instead of reacting, you regulate.
Instead of retreating, you engage.

Breaking the cycle also requires humility—admitting when you are wrong, apologizing without conditions, and listening without defending. It means choosing understanding over being right and connection over emotional control.

This work is not easy. But the alternative—carrying resentment, repeating painful patterns, and losing meaningful relationships—is far more costly.

When you choose courage, honesty, and emotional maturity, conflict becomes a pathway to healing, deeper connection, and lasting growth.

This is how cycles end.
This is how relationships are rebuilt.
This is how emotional safety is restored.

Reflection Activity

Boy, oh boy… this one hits home.

There is something profoundly freeing about healing, learning from your mistakes, and walking forward with a lighter heart. It took me years—decades, even—to fully understand how unresolved conflict shaped my relationships and emotional patterns.

To explain, I have to return briefly to my childhood. I grew up in a home where spousal abuse was part of the environment. Conflict was loud, violent, and frightening. But just as often, it was avoided—silenced, ignored, and never processed. Pain simmered beneath the surface, unresolved and unnamed.

What did I learn?

I learned to avoid conflict.

Period.

But avoidance doesn't make conflict disappear. It stores it. And stored pain eventually demands release—often in damaging ways.

It took years for me to unlearn that survival strategy. Years to build emotional safety inside myself. Years to learn how to say, *"Something isn't right here. Can we talk?"*

That shift changed my relationships. But my fear of conflict still cost me important connections along the way.

And this pattern shows up powerfully in the workplace.

We avoid hard conversations. We stay silent in meetings. We suppress frustration. Over time, resentment builds, emotional safety erodes, and burnout follows. Fear-based communication creates toxic cultures.

Whether at home or at work, conflict requires emotional regulation, clarity, courage, and compassion.

Practice:

Think of a conflict you've been avoiding—personal or professional.
Take a few slow breaths.
Write how you want to approach it with emotional clarity, honesty, and courage.

Regulate your attitude.
Check your assumptions.
Clarify your expectations.

And move toward healing.

Ch 3D. Selfishness or Self-Centeredness:

A successful relationship—whether personal or professional—thrives on mutual respect, empathy, and a healthy balance of give and take. But what happens when one person becomes so consumed with their own desires, needs, or goals that they neglect the other? That imbalance doesn't stay quiet. It breeds frustration, emotional distance, feelings of abandonment, and eventually the breakdown of trust. Selfishness slowly erodes the foundation of connection, leaving the neglected person feeling invisible, unimportant, and uncared for.

But here is the deeper truth: selfishness is rarely the real issue. Underneath the behavior is almost always something older, deeper, and more complex. **Self-centeredness is often a survival strategy**—a nervous-system response shaped by past experiences, unhealed wounds, and early environments. When the brain learns that needs won't be met consistently, it often shifts into protection mode: *secure yourself first.*

Think about an only child who grew up navigating the world with no real practice in sharing or considering others. In the early years of life—before school, peer conflict, and social correction—an only child's reality can be centered on self. Not because they're "bad," but because that was the world they knew. That mindset can follow them into adulthood unless intentional work is done to grow beyond it.

Now consider someone whose childhood was marked by struggle. Maybe there was never enough food, never enough stability, never enough love. Clothes were handed down, not new. The house may have been filled with chaos, addiction, or neglect. When survival mode becomes a child's daily norm, self-preservation becomes their default attitude. That same survival wiring can show up later as selfishness—not because they want to neglect others, but because their brain learned early on that the safest option was to take care of themselves first.

Or imagine the child who grew up fourth out of six siblings, always squeezed between the needs of the older kids and the demands of the younger ones. They may have spent their entire childhood feeling unseen, unheard, and overshadowed. As adults, they might cling to attention, validation, or affirmation—not out of ego, but out of a lifelong nervous-system hunger to finally feel noticed. Their "selfishness" is actually the echo of a child who vowed, *I will never be invisible again.*

What I am trying to illuminate is this: selfishness and self-centeredness are not always malicious. **They are signals.** They point to an underlying cause—an attitude shaped by years of unmet needs, pain, or threat response. When we recognize that attitude is the root, we stop seeing the person as the problem and start seeing the story behind the behavior.

And now that we understand the root, we can help the person we care about grow. We can approach them with compassion instead of judgment, honesty instead of resentment, and understanding instead of anger. We can restore our relationships. We can rebuild trust. We can strengthen our teams.

Because once we address the root—not just the behavior—we make room for healing, growth, and connection to flourish again.

"Selfishness is not living as one wishes to live, it is asking others to live as one wishes to live." — Oscar Wilde

Selfishness or self-centeredness primarily aligns with attitude, though it's often reinforced by expectations and assumptions in subtle, damaging ways.

Selfishness or Self-Centeredness and Attitude:
The Core of Self-Centeredness

Selfishness is not simply a behavior—it is an attitude. It is a mindset that turns a person inward and keeps their focus centered on their own comfort, needs, and desires. This inward posture shrinks the relational space until only one person's world matters. And for many, this attitude didn't appear in adulthood; it began in youth, shaped by early experiences, family dynamics, or environments where they had to think about themselves first just to feel secure, safe, or seen.

Sometimes this attitude grows from entitlement—the belief that one deserves more attention or consideration than others. Other times, it stems from a lack of empathy, where a person was never taught or modeled how to see beyond themselves or recognize how their actions affect the people around them. In some cases, the attitude shows up through a need for control, often rooted in childhood chaos or inconsistency, making personal comfort feel like the only safe anchor.

Richard J. Foster captures this disposition vividly: "The self-centered man will always expect nothing but praise… and will resent anything less." That resentment surfaces whenever the world refuses to revolve around them, creating tension in personal and professional relationships alike.

These attitude-driven traits—entitlement, limited empathy, and the need for control—are what truly disrupt relationships. They strain friendships, burden romantic partnerships, and weaken workplace culture. When left unchallenged, this attitude erodes trust and connection.

But when we recognize that self-centeredness is rooted in attitude—and that this attitude often began long before adulthood—we gain the ability to address it at its source, support healing, and rebuild healthier, more balanced relationships and teams.

Selfishness or Self-Centeredness and Expectations: *The Demand for Special Treatment*

Self-centeredness rarely appears in isolation. It usually carries with it an entire world of expectations—expectations that revolve around the belief that other people exist to meet your needs. When a person operates from a self-focused attitude, they begin to assume that support, attention, effort, and accommodation should flow toward them automatically. These expectations often develop long before adulthood, shaped by early patterns where their needs were either always prioritized or constantly ignored. But by the time this attitude reaches relationships, the damage can be profound.

Selfishness often disguises itself behind these one-sided expectations: the belief that others should stay consistent, patient, loyal, and attentive no matter how little you offer in return. From this mindset, relationships stop being mutual exchanges of care and begin functioning like emotional vending machines—insert nothing, expect everything.

In romantic relationships, this shows up as expecting a partner to absorb your moods, soothe your insecurities, or carry the emotional load while you give minimal effort. You expect understanding even when you offer none. You want forgiveness on demand, but apology feels beneath you. This imbalance eventually drains the relationship of tenderness, safety, and connection.

In friendships, self-centered expectations cast an even broader shadow. Someone who is driven by their own internal world assumes their friends should always make time, always show support, always initiate, and always be available—regardless of how inconsistent or disengaged they themselves may be. Over time, the friend who is constantly giving begins to feel unappreciated and emotionally overdrawn. The bond becomes heavy because only one person is carrying it.

In the workplace, this same attitude shows up when someone wants recognition without responsibility, or advancement without accountability. They may expect flexibility from their team but refuse to offer the same. They want praise for effort they never actually contributed. These expectations, fueled by a self-centered attitude, fracture collaboration and create an unhealthy team culture where resentment grows and trust disappears.

Whenever expectations revolve around a single person's wants, the relationship—whether at home or at work—loses balance. It becomes strained, uneven, and eventually unsustainable. People stop feeling valued and start feeling used. Emotional generosity is replaced with emotional depletion.

"Expecting others to make you happy is the surest way to be disappointed." — Dr. Wayne Dyer

Selfishness or Self-Centeredness and Assumptions: *Justifying Self-Interest*

Self-centeredness rarely operates without a story attached to it. The attitude doesn't stand alone—it is fueled, defended, and sustained by a set of assumptions that make the self-focused behavior feel reasonable, necessary, or even noble. These assumptions become the internal script a person rehearses to protect their ego, justify their choices, and silence their guilt. But while these assumptions may offer short-term comfort, they create long-term damage in relationships.

One of the most common assumptions behind self-centered behavior is the belief that "If I don't put myself first, no one else will." This mindset often originates from childhood environments where needs were ignored or dismissed. Over time, the person learns to depend solely on themselves—and later carries that survival strategy into relationships where it no longer belongs. What once kept them safe now keeps them distant.

Another assumption quietly feeding self-centeredness is the idea that "They don't need me as much as I need them." This belief creates emotional detachment, allowing the person to avoid showing up fully in relationships. It minimizes the importance of reciprocity and makes neglect feel justified. But beneath this assumption is usually a deeper fear: the fear of being inadequate, rejected, or unable to meet the other person's needs.

Then there is the assumption rooted in cynicism: "Everyone else is out for themselves—so I should be too." This belief closes the heart off to vulnerability and generosity. It creates a world where trust feels dangerous, kindness feels foolish, and cooperation feels optional. People who carry this assumption often experienced betrayal or inconsistency early in life, and they learned to protect themselves by mirroring the selfishness they once witnessed.

These assumptions act like armor—thick enough to protect, but also thick enough to isolate. They soothe the ego but sever the connection. They give the illusion of strength while actually reinforcing weakness. And most importantly, they keep relationships from forming the mutual, honest, and emotionally present foundation they require to thrive.

When someone believes these assumptions, their selfishness doesn't feel like selfishness. It feels like logic. It feels justified. It feels safe. But to the people around them, it feels hurtful, dismissive, and invalidating. These assumptions widen the emotional distance and make empathy nearly impossible.

The work, then, is to expose the assumptions for what they really are: protective narratives created by past experiences—not truths that should govern present relationships. When we challenge the assumptions behind self-centeredness, we interrupt the cycle and open the door for humility, empathy, and mutual care to take root.

This is where transformation begins—when self-protection gives way to self-awareness, and assumptions are replaced with truth, connection, and intentional growth.

"Assumptions are the termites of relationships." — Henry Winkler

Breaking the Cycle

Breaking the cycle of selfishness requires far more than noticing the behavior—it demands the willingness to confront the internal forces that shaped it. Self-centeredness is not random. It grows out of an attitude built in childhood, reinforced by one-sided expectations, and protected by assumptions that justify putting oneself first. Because its roots run deep, the process of transformation must also go deep. This is not surface-level work; it is heart work, mindset work, and character work.

The first step in breaking the cycle is shifting the attitude that has governed your relationships. This means choosing humility over entitlement, empathy over isolation, and mutual benefit over personal gain. Self-centeredness says, "I deserve more." Humility says, "We both matter here."

When you learn to value shared success, shared responsibility, and shared emotional labor, your presence becomes safer and more dependable for the people around you. Attitude is the soil where all behavior grows—change the soil, and the fruit changes too.

Breaking the cycle also requires confronting the expectations that have been silently driving your interactions. Instead of expecting others to meet your needs without effort from you, you begin to understand that love, friendship, and teamwork thrive only when both sides contribute. Healthy expectations recognize that emotional support, consideration, and generosity must flow in both directions. One-sided expectations collapse relationships; shared expectations strengthen them.

Then comes the work of challenging the assumptions that have been defending your selfishness from the inside out. The old stories—*"No one will take care of me," "They don't need me," "Everyone else is self-focused anyway"—*must be brought into the light and examined honestly. These assumptions were formed to protect you, but they have also been limiting you. True connection is built not through self-preservation but through shared responsibility, vulnerability, and trust. When assumptions are replaced with truth, relational healing becomes possible.

Albert Einstein once wrote, "Only a life lived for others is a life worthwhile." This is not a call to neglect yourself—it is a call to recognize that meaning is found in connection, not isolation. Selfishness isolates. It builds walls, not bridges. It creates distance, not intimacy. It prioritizes the individual at the expense of the relationship. But empathy softens the heart. Humility widens the perspective. Service anchors the relationship in stability and trust.

Breaking the cycle of self-centeredness means choosing connection over comfort, accountability over excuses, and growth over old patterns. It means recognizing the needs of others without dismissing your own. It means becoming the kind of person who contributes rather than consumes, who listens rather than dominates, who collaborates rather than controls.

This is the work that restores relationships. This is the work that strengthens families, friendships, and teams. This is the work that transforms your character and reshapes your impact. And while it is hard, it is holy work—because on the other side of the cycle is a version of you capable of deeper love, healthier relationships, and a more fulfilling life.

This is how the cycle ends. This is how healing begins.

Reflection Activity

Now, let's be real. You're reading this because you want to strengthen your relationships and own your part in the ones that didn't work. That takes courage.

And let's be honest—we've all had selfish moments. If just thinking about this section makes you uneasy, you're not alone. That discomfort might be your ego talking. But growth doesn't happen in comfort zones.

"We don't see things as they are, we see them as we are."
— Anaïs Nin

I've always seen myself as a giver. I became the matriarch of my family before I even understood what that meant. I served, I nurtured, I led. So, do I really want to admit to moments of selfishness?

Yes—because healing requires honesty.

One moment that still humbles me happened when I was in a leadership role. I had inherited a dysfunctional team and was tasked with leading a turnaround. I made swift, necessary changes. Strategically, I was right. But relationally—I missed the mark.

I didn't stop to consider the emotional whiplash those changes caused. I assumed my clarity of vision was enough. It wasn't.

I had to sit in that discomfort and take accountability. My intentions were good—but good intentions don't excuse harmful impact.

"Intentions may pave the road, but it's the walk that shapes the journey." — Unknown

That moment taught me a lesson I'll never forget: leadership—and all relationships—must be rooted in service, not control. In the *us*, not the *me*.

So now, I turn the mirror to you. Reflect:

Activity: When have you let your self-centeredness, assumptions, or expectations hurt a relationship? What will you do differently moving forward?

Ch 3E. Jealousy and Insecurity

Jealousy and insecurity—whether in love, in family dynamics, or in the workplace—have the power to poison even the strongest connections. When insecurity creeps in, it gives birth to suspicion, control, comparison, and quiet competition. These emotions weaken trust, distort perspective, and fracture relationships in ways that feel personal, even when they aren't. Theodore Roosevelt captured this reality perfectly when he said, "Comparison is the thief of joy." What he didn't say is that comparison is also the thief of peace, trust, and emotional stability.

At their core, jealousy and insecurity are fueled by assumptions—false stories we create in moments of fear. When someone is insecure, the mind begins forming narratives that feel true even if they have no evidence behind them:
"Their success means I'm behind."
"If they're paying attention to someone else, I must not matter."

These stories don't have to be accurate to do damage. They only have to be believed. And once believed, they shape reactions, tone, behavior, and emotional intensity.

But as heavy and disruptive as jealousy and insecurity can be, they are **not** the true destroyers of relationships. They are symptoms, not the root. It may seem like your jealous partner or colleague is constantly throwing tantrums about fairness, or picking apart situations with a magnifying glass, or interrogating every detail as if they're searching for hidden betrayal. But the truth is this: their outward behavior is the surface-level expression of something deeper—something older—something rooted in attitude.

The jealous outbursts, the controlling tendencies, the constant comparing…these are reflections of an internal attitude shaped long before the present relationship, often beginning in childhood or early adulthood. Underneath jealousy is an attitude of *"I am not enough."* Underneath insecurity is an attitude of *"I will be replaced."* Underneath comparison is an attitude of *"There isn't room for both of us to win."*

These attitudes form from early experiences—being overlooked, ignored, replaced, compared to siblings, or constantly criticized. Or they form in adulthood after betrayal, abandonment, or workplace environments where competition was valued more than collaboration. Whatever the origin, the attitude becomes the lens they look through. And when the lens is distorted, every interaction becomes distorted with it.

The point is not to excuse the behavior but to understand it. Because once we understand it, we can deal with the true root instead of just reacting to the symptoms. Jealousy and insecurity appear to be the problem, but beneath the surface, the real issue is **the** attitude that gives them power. And once you shift the attitude, the behaviors lose their grip.

Jealousy and Insecurity and Assumptions:

The Root of Jealousy and Insecurity

Jealousy and insecurity do not appear out of thin air—they grow in the places where our assumptions are loudest and our clarity is weakest. Insecurity thrives in the shadows of what we imagine, fear, or interpret without ever confirming the truth. The mind fills in the gaps long before evidence appears. And once assumptions take root, they create emotional realities powerful enough to shape how we act, speak, and react.

In romantic relationships, insecurity often shows up as assuming a partner is unfaithful or losing interest—even when there is no proof. A delayed text, a change in tone, or a busy schedule becomes "evidence" of betrayal. But what is really happening is not an issue of fidelity—it is an issue of the internal story the insecure partner believes about themselves: *"I'm not enough. I'm replaceable. I'm one mistake away from being abandoned."* When the assumption becomes the narrative, jealousy becomes the reaction.

In friendships, these assumptions take on a quieter form. Someone begins believing they've been excluded, ignored, or replaced without ever asking a single question. A missed invitation, a conversation they weren't part of, or a photo posted on social media becomes a sign of rejection. The assumption isn't just about the friend—it is about the silent fear humming beneath the surface: *"I don't matter as much as I thought."*

And in the workplace, insecurity shows up with even sharper edges. A colleague receiving praise, a supervisor offering someone else an opportunity, or a team member being given additional responsibility becomes a trigger for assumptions of inferiority: *"They're better than me. I don't measure up. Leadership prefers them."* These assumptions lead to self-doubt, resentment, and emotional withdrawal, none of which are based on truth—but all of which feel painfully real.

These mental scripts—created not by truth, but by fear—quickly become emotional realities. And emotional realities drive behaviors. A person who *feels* replaced will act guarded. A person who *assumes* betrayal will act suspicious. A person who *believes* they are less competent will shrink, retreat, or overcompensate. The damage doesn't come from what is true, but from what is believed.

Tariq Ramadan's words echo loudly here: *"You must learn to let go of assumptions. They are the enemies of truth."* Assumptions do more than distort truth—they become the fuel that intensifies insecurity and the spark that ignites jealousy. They pull people into false conclusions, unnecessary conflict, and emotional exhaustion.

But here is the key insight: jealousy and insecurity are not the core problem. They are the visible symptoms of deeper attitudes shaped long before the current relationship or environment. The attitude of *"I'm not enough," "I will be abandoned,"* or *"There is not enough room for me to succeed"* gives assumptions their power.

Once we strip away the assumptions, the insecurity loses its foundation. And once we challenge the attitude beneath them, jealousy loses its grip entirely.

Jealousy and Insecurity and Attitude: *The Mindset That Fuels Jealousy*

Jealousy does not begin with circumstances—it begins with attitude. It grows from the internal mindset we carry long before any outside situation arises. When our attitude is shaped by lack, fear, or comparison, jealousy has fertile ground to grow. This mindset interprets love, success, attention, or opportunity as limited resources, as if what someone else receives automatically takes something away from us. When we see the world through this lens, admiration slowly turns into resentment, and connection quietly shifts into competition.

A scarcity mindset is one of the primary attitudes fueling jealousy. This attitude whispers, *"There isn't enough for me."* In relationships, that might sound like, *"If they give attention to someone else, there's less left for me."* At work: *"If someone else excels, I must be falling behind."* In families: *"If they celebrate one child, the others must be overlooked."* But this mindset is built on fear, not truth. Love is not finite. Opportunity is not rationed. And blessings are not distributed like limited supplies.

Peace begins to return when we remember that God's blessings are never scarce—what He appoints for one person never subtracts from what He intends for another. Heaven does not run out. Favor does not have a quota. Destiny is not a competition. When we shift this internal attitude, jealousy loses much of its grip because the heart stops believing it has something to lose.

Another root attitude behind jealousy is low self-worth—the deep belief that you are not enough, or that you are always one moment away from being replaced, abandoned, or overlooked. When someone carries this internal posture, every compliment someone else receives feels like a threat. Every success someone else enjoys feels like evidence of their own inadequacy. But jealousy in these moments is not about the other person at all—it is about the fragile relationship we have with ourselves.

A third attitude that fuels jealousy is a distrustful outlook—a mindset shaped by past betrayal, abandonment, or inconsistency. When distrust becomes the default attitude, people begin interpreting neutral moments as danger signs. They expect betrayal even when there is no evidence. They brace for disappointment before anything disappointing has occurred. Suspicion becomes the lens through which everything is viewed.

Brené Brown captured this reality when she wrote, *"Jealousy is a hunger that rots the soul."* It rots because it devours peace, confidence, gratitude, and clarity. It starves relationships of trust. It drains joy from personal achievements. And most painfully, it blinds us to the blessings already present.

When we do not trust ourselves, we struggle to trust others. When we fear losing love, we cling too tightly. When we fear losing opportunities, we compare too quickly. Jealousy becomes the default lens—distorting interactions, damaging relationships, and exhausting the heart.

But the moment we address the **attitude** beneath jealousy—scarcity, low self-worth, or distrust—the entire narrative begins to shift. We see others not as threats but as partners. We celebrate instead of competing. We trust instead of obsessing. We appreciate instead of resenting.

Jealousy and Insecurity and Expectations: *The Pressure to Measure Up*

Jealousy and expectations are often born from the same soil — the quiet belief that love, attention, or success must be earned or compared. Jealousy whispers that someone else's gain is our loss, while unhealthy expectations convince us that others should instinctively meet needs we've never voiced. Together, they create emotional tension that clouds our perception of both ourselves and those we care about.

When expectations are unrealistic, we begin to script relationships rather than experience them, assigning roles that others never agreed to play. When jealousy enters, it distorts that script, making genuine connection feel like competition. Over time, we measure affection by how much someone gives, instead of how deeply we understand.

Freedom from this cycle begins with awareness — recognizing that neither jealousy nor expectation defines love. Love thrives in clarity, honesty, and acceptance. When we communicate what we need without demanding perfection, and celebrate others without comparing our journey to theirs, we shift from scarcity to abundance. In that space, jealousy loses its power, and expectations evolve into mutual understanding rather than silent disappointment.

In the workplace, the same dynamic quietly unfolds. Jealousy shows up as resentment toward a colleague's promotion or recognition, while unhealthy expectations appear as assumptions that others should notice our effort or operate by our standards. Both create silent divides within teams. When success is seen as scarce, collaboration erodes and comparison replaces contribution. The healthiest workplaces, like healthy relationships, are built on transparency and shared purpose. When we clarify expectations, celebrate others' wins, and trust that there is enough opportunity for everyone, we replace envy with empowerment. Professional growth becomes collective, not competitive — and the workplace transforms from a field of rivalry into a community of respect.

- Expecting a partner to constantly validate your worth.
- Expecting constant inclusion from friends or coworkers.
- Expecting yourself to always outperform others.

When those expectations aren't met, resentment and self-doubt follow. "Don't trade your authenticity for someone else's approval." — Unknown

Breaking the Cycle

Breaking the cycle of jealousy and insecurity doesn't start with fixing other people—it starts with being honest about what is happening inside of you. Jealousy and insecurity feel like reactions to *them*—their promotion, their attention, their message, their success—but at the deepest level, they are reflections of your own attitude, assumptions, and expectations. You cannot heal what you only blame. The moment you decide to take responsibility for your inner world instead of arranging your outer world around your fears, the cycle has already begun to crack.

The first step is awareness. You cannot change what you refuse to name. When jealousy rises—when your chest tightens as you scroll, when you replay a conversation, when you feel yourself judging or minimizing someone else—pause and ask: *What story am I telling myself right now?* Maybe it sounds like, "I'm falling behind," "I'm not enough," "They're going to leave," or "I don't matter unless I'm chosen first." Instead of treating these as facts, recognize them as *assumptions shaped by fear*, not truth rooted in reality. Naming the story loosens its power. You move from *"This is what's happening"* to *"This is what I'm afraid is happening."* That shift alone opens a door for healing.

The second step is challenging your assumptions. Jealousy feeds off untested narratives. When you assume your partner is uninterested, your friend is done with you, or your coworker is more valued, you begin to act as if those fears are confirmed—pulling back, lashing out, becoming cold or clingy. To break the cycle, you must become willing to ask instead of assume. That might sound like, "When you pulled away earlier, I told myself you were losing interest. Is that what's really going on?" or "I noticed I wasn't included and I started to assume I don't matter. Can we talk about that?" This is vulnerable work, but it is also mature work. It trades silent suspicion for honest conversation. You may discover that some fears are unfounded—or, if something *is* off, at least you are responding to truth instead of imagination.

The third step is reframing your attitude from scarcity to abundance. Scarcity says, "If they have it, I can't." Abundance says, "There is room for both of us to be seen, loved, and successful." Scarcity makes everything a competition: their compliment is your threat; their win is your loss. Abundance remembers that what God has ordained for one person does not cancel what He has ordained for another. Love is not a limited inventory. Opportunity is not a single chair at a tiny table. Destiny is not a race where only one person can finish. When you begin to consciously bless others instead of secretly resenting them, you retrain your heart. Try this: when jealousy flares, deliberately pray for the person you're tempted to envy. Thank God for what He's doing in their life, and then thank Him in advance for what He is still writing in yours. Over time, your spirit learns that celebration is safer than comparison.

The fourth step is resetting expectations—of others and of yourself. Jealousy and insecurity intensify when we expect people to read our minds, heal our history, or constantly reassure us in ways we've never clearly communicated. It also grows when we demand perfection from ourselves: always being chosen, always being praised, always outperforming. Breaking the cycle means moving from unspoken, unrealistic expectations to clear, healthy ones. In relationships, that might sound like, "When you affirm me, it helps me feel secure. I'd love to hear that from you more often," instead of punishing them when they don't guess what you need. In friendships and at work, it might mean acknowledging: "I want to be included and recognized, but I also know I have a responsibility to communicate, show up, and contribute." Expectations rooted in reality invite mutual understanding; expectations rooted in fantasy guarantee disappointment.

Fifth, do the internal work of rebuilding self-worth. Jealousy and insecurity lose their grip as you develop a more grounded sense of who you are—apart from titles, attention, or comparison. This might include therapy, spiritual mentorship, journaling, or intentional practices like listing your strengths, naming your values, and reminding yourself of your identity in God, not in people's responses. When you begin to believe, *"I am enough, even when I'm not the favorite,"* your nervous system stops treating every perceived shift in attention as an emergency. The less you fear being replaced, the less you feel compelled to compete.

In the workplace, breaking the cycle means choosing collaboration over quiet rivalry. Instead of shrinking when someone else shines—or subtly undermining their success—look for ways to learn from them, support them, and grow alongside them. Ask yourself, "What can I contribute to this team that no one else brings?" and "How can I honor their strengths without minimizing my own?" When expectations and goals are clarified, when success is defined as *collective advancement rather than individual dominance*, jealousy has nowhere to hide. Teams that talk openly about performance, recognition, and growth paths remove much of the secrecy that fuels insecurity.

Finally, breaking the cycle requires ongoing courage, not a one-time decision. You will still feel twinges of jealousy. You will still have insecure thoughts. The difference is what you do with them. Instead of letting them drive your behavior, you now have tools: pause, name the story, challenge the assumption, adjust your attitude, reset expectations, and return to truth. You may even say it plainly to yourself: *"This is jealousy talking. This is insecurity talking. I don't have to obey it."* Over time, the volume of those voices lowers, and the voice of peace—grounded in confidence, clarity, and compassion—grows stronger.

Jealousy and insecurity don't have to write the story of your relationships or your work life. When you tend to the root—your attitude, assumptions, and expectations—you stop reacting from fear and begin responding from wholeness. The same places where envy once lived can become spaces of gratitude. The same moments where you used to compete can become opportunities to connect. And slowly, steadily, the cycle that once poisoned your connections becomes the very place where growth, healing, and deeper trust take root.

Reflection Activity

Let me speak directly to those carrying the weight of betrayal. If you've been cheated on, abandoned, or overlooked for a promotion you were promised, you may find yourself expecting every future relationship or opportunity to end the same way.

And honestly? I've been there.

My first experience with love ended in heartbreak... and motherhood at fifteen. For years afterward, every relationship carried the imprint of that wound. I assumed betrayal was inevitable. And while betrayal did happen again, I eventually realized something important: it wasn't the betrayal that drained me—it was my insecurity and jealousy. My own assumptions haunted me more deeply than the heartbreak itself.

"Insecurity is loud. Confidence is quiet." — Unknown

But something shifted. God's love broke through. One day, I finally chose to believe what He says about me: *I am enough.* That single decision released me from a mental prison I had lived in for years.

I began recognizing how hard I worked and became more vocal when opportunities for promotion came up. In my personal relationships, I realized how much I bring to the table—starting with the fact that I am nurturing and supportive, and every healthy relationship needs both. I simply became more aware of who I was and more willing to express it, instead of shrinking into meekness and insecurity. Now, I live by these truths:

• At work, I am enough. I own my growth and I own my worth.

• In love, I am enough. If he can't see that, he is free to go. God will never leave me nor forsake me.

• In friendships, I am enough. Even if I can't meet every need, I rest knowing I gave my best.

And guess what? When I embraced this mindset, every one of my relationships improved because I began showing up with confidence, peace, and self-love.

Now it's your turn.
Write it. Say it. Believe it: I AM ENOUGH.

Now reflect:
Where have you felt like you weren't enough?
How do you plan to show up differently now?

"Owning our story and loving ourselves through that process is the bravest thing that we'll ever do." — Brené Brown

Ch3F. Lack of Empathy:

Empathy is the capacity to feel *with* another person—to tune into their emotional state, understand their experience, and recognize their humanity. When empathy is absent, meaningful connection cannot survive. It is the anchor of every healthy relationship, and when it slips away, the bond begins to loosen. Without empathy, people stop relating heart-to-heart and begin relating task-to-task. Others become inconveniences, irritations, or background noise instead of individuals with real emotions and real needs.

What follows is not always intentional harm; often, it is emotional shutdown. Neuroscience tells us that when the nervous system is overwhelmed by stress, threat, burnout, or unresolved emotional pain, the brain shifts into survival mode — and empathy is one of the first capacities to go offline. The body prioritizes self-protection over connection. The result is not cruelty, but emotional numbness. Yet the impact is the same. A relationship without empathy slowly starves.

It is unsettling to watch someone who once cared deeply become withdrawn, guarded, or emotionally unavailable. That shift rarely happens overnight. Instead, people lose empathy in small moments—after repeated disappointment, chronic stress, emotional exhaustion, or relational injury. Over time, the nervous system learns to stay guarded rather than open. And once empathy fades, emotional presence fades with it

At its core, empathy is a nervous system posture of safety. It is choosing to stay emotionally available rather than emotionally armored. It is listening to understand rather than listening to defend. It is seeing beyond your own experience long enough to truly grasp what someone else is carrying. Empathy does not require agreement or solutions; it requires regulation, presence, and emotional availability.

When empathy disappears from a relationship—whether at home, among friends, or in the workplace—we lose one of the most powerful tools we have for connection, healing, and trust.

"Too often we underestimate the power of a touch, a smile, a kind word… all of which have the potential to turn a life around." — Leo Buscaglia

A lack of empathy almost always begins with **attitude** — how we regard people, how much emotional space we allow for their experience, and how open we are to perspectives beyond our own. But it does not stop there.

Assumptions distort our interpretations, and expectations shape how we believe others should feel, behave, or heal.

Together, these three forces — attitude, assumptions, and expectations — quietly dismantle relationships long before anyone notices what is slipping away.

And this is critical to understand: it is not a lack of empathy that destroys relationships — it is the three silent relationship destroyers that shut empathy down.

Let's break it down.

Lack of Empathy and Attitude: *The Core of Emotional Disconnection*

Empathy may be rooted in the heart, but the soil it grows in is **attitude**. The way we regard people — the value we assign to their feelings, the dignity we grant their experience, the emotional space we allow — determines whether empathy can flourish. You cannot extend what your nervous system does not feel safe offering.

When empathy is missing, it is rarely because someone lacks the capacity to care. More often, their **attitude has shifted into self-protection mode.** Their nervous system has decided it is safer to disengage than to remain emotionally open.

This shows up in subtle but powerful ways. Some people begin moving through life as the central character in every interaction, filtering everything through their own emotional needs. When this inward posture takes over, relationships become one-sided. Conversations become transactional. Other people's pain becomes interruption rather than invitation.

For others, judgment becomes the barrier. Instead of listening, they evaluate. Instead of understanding, they label. Their internal narrative becomes: *"This isn't that serious," "They're too sensitive," or "They should be over this by now."* These judgments are not signs of strength — they are signs of emotional distancing.

Then there is emotional numbness — the quiet, dangerous form of disconnection. Often mistaken for calm, it is actually emotional shutdown. Burnout, unresolved trauma, chronic stress, and repeated disappointment can teach the nervous system to disengage as a form of survival. The result is emotional detachment that leaves others feeling unseen and alone.

Each of these attitudes closes the door to empathy long before words are exchanged. Empathy does not require solutions — it requires emotional presence. And presence is only possible when the nervous system feels safe enough to stay open.

As Alfred Adler wrote, "Empathy is seeing with the eyes of another, listening with the ears of another, and feeling with the heart of another."

When attitude honors humanity, empathy becomes natural. When attitude shifts into self-protection, empathy becomes optional — and relationships cannot survive when empathy is optional.

Lack of Empathy and Assumptions: *Emotional Shortcuts That Kill Connection*

A lack of empathy does not always stem from cruelty. Often, it comes from **mental shortcuts** — assumptions that allow us to avoid emotional labor.

Instead of slowing down to understand, people jump to conclusions:

- *If it doesn't affect me, it can't be that serious.*
- *They're overreacting.*
- *They should have moved on by now.*

These thoughts feel efficient — but they are relational poison. Assumptions bypass curiosity and shut down compassion. They allow people to stay emotionally comfortable while others feel emotionally abandoned.

Assumptions silence vulnerability. They replace connection with conclusion.

Neuroscience tells us the brain craves efficiency and certainty. Assumptions provide both — but at the cost of empathy. Rather than engaging emotionally, the brain chooses narrative closure. The story feels safer than the uncertainty of connection.

But healing does not happen through conclusions. Healing happens through curiosity.

If pain could simply be "gotten over," trauma therapy wouldn't exist. Grief wouldn't linger. Emotional wounds wouldn't echo across decades. And workplaces wouldn't be filled with silent burnout and emotional fatigue.

Assumptions may feel protective, but they are intimacy killers. They block understanding, silence vulnerability, and starve relationships of emotional safety.

Lack of Empathy and Expectations: *The Demand for Emotional Uniformity*

One of the quietest destroyers of empathy is the expectation that others should feel, react, or recover **the way we do.**

This expectation creates emotional rigidity — the belief that there is a correct timeline, correct reaction, or correct emotional response. When others deviate from that script, frustration replaces compassion.

In relationships, this shows up as emotional correction rather than emotional care:
"Calm down."
"Don't take it so personally."
"You're too sensitive."

In friendships, it appears as emotional impatience:
"Why are you still upset about that?"
"You should be past this by now."

In the workplace, emotional uniformity becomes policy:
"Leave your personal life at the door."
"Be professional."

But nervous systems don't operate on command. Humans cannot simply switch emotions off. Expecting emotional sameness denies nervous system reality.

When we expect emotional uniformity, we deny emotional humanity.

Empathy thrives when we allow emotional diversity. People heal differently. Process differently. Feel differently. And when we release the demand that others mirror us, connection becomes possible again.

Breaking the Cycle: *Rebuilding the E in Heart*

Restoring empathy is not about becoming more emotional. It is about becoming **more regulated, more present, and more curious.**

Empathy grows where emotional safety lives.

The first step is **awareness** — recognizing when your nervous system is pulling inward instead of reaching outward. When judgment replaces curiosity. When emotional fatigue replaces compassion. Awareness interrupts autopilot.

The second step is **curiosity.** Asking:
What might they be carrying that I cannot see?

This single question softens defenses and reopens connection.

The third step is **regulation.** Empathy cannot exist when your nervous system is overwhelmed. Leaders, partners, parents, and professionals must learn emotional regulation — because regulated nervous systems create safe relational environments.

The fourth step is **release of emotional uniformity.** People do not need to heal on your timeline, feel through your temperament, or process through your lens. Emotional diversity is not dysfunction — it is humanity.

And finally, empathy returns when we choose **presence over fixing, compassion over correction, and connection over control.**

Empathy is not about solutions.
It is about *being seen.*

Empathy interrupts the AAE™ survival cascade.
Empathy softens attitude.
Empathy clarifies assumptions.
Empathy recalibrates expectations.

And when empathy returns, trust, safety, and healing follow.

Ch3G Toxic Behavior and Abuse

Some behaviors go far beyond miscommunication, irritation, or simple human flaws. They cross a line into territory that is destructive, dangerous, and deeply damaging. Manipulation. Emotional abuse. Physical abuse. Controlling behavior. These are not misunderstandings or "rough patches"—they are warning sirens, announcing that something within the relationship has fractured in a way that may be irreparable.

Toxic dynamics do more than hurt—they instill fear. They breed shame. They erode confidence and trust. They slowly create a power imbalance where one person feels small, cornered, or stripped of their voice. Before long, the person on the receiving end begins doubting their own worth, their own intuition, even their own reality. And that's what toxic behavior is designed to do—**disorient the nervous system**, silence, and weaken.

But toxic behavior and abuse don't appear suddenly or all at once. They unfold in stages. The first time it happens, you feel jolted—shocked that someone you care about could act this way. You try to shake it off. You tell yourself they were stressed, upset, or "just having a moment." A part of you wants to dismiss it, but a deeper part knows the truth: this moment should not be ignored, minimized, or brushed aside.

Then it happens again. The second incident hits differently because now you can't pretend it was accidental. This is the moment when fear quietly creeps in. The awareness rises in your chest: I need to do something.

But instead of acting, many people freeze. They rationalize. They offer excuses. They hope things will improve. They fear confrontation. And sometimes the fear is even bigger—What if leaving means losing everything? What if you have to leave your job, your marriage, your church, your community group… the spaces that have anchored your identity and belonging? That fear can be paralyzing.

This is survival physiology at work—when threat feels real, the brain often chooses freeze or fawn before it chooses fight or flight.

Toxicity isn't random—it has roots. It is often born from a destructive attitude, supported by false assumptions, and sustained by unhealthy expectations. These internal forces become invisible threads, tightening themselves around the relationship until neither person can breathe. By the time the damage becomes visible, those threads have already been tightening for months or years—**and the body often senses it long before the mind can name it.**

And while not every toxic behavior qualifies as abuse, every abusive behavior is toxic at its core. They all operate on the same foundation: someone believes their power, comfort, or control is more important than another person's safety and dignity.

Toxic behavior might begin with raised voices or emotional manipulation, but it rarely ends there if left unchecked. The pattern deepens. The control grows. The fear intensifies. And the relationship slowly becomes a place of survival instead of connection.

The purpose of this chapter is not to blame the victim or justify the abuser—it is to illuminate the roots of this behavior so healing, boundaries, and escape routes can be identified. Because toxic behavior is not simply about what is happening on the surface—it's about the mindset beneath it. And unless the internal attitude driving this behavior is confronted and transformed, the cycle will continue.

You are not imagining it. You don't deserve it.
And it is not your job to "tolerate your way" into safety.

The rest of this section will explore how attitude, assumptions, and expectations contribute to toxic dynamics—and what must shift to break free from them.

Toxic Behavior & Attitude:
Where the Destruction Truly Begins

Toxic behavior doesn't start with the behavior you see—it starts with the attitude you can't see. The outward explosion, the manipulation, the yelling, the intimidation… those are symptoms. The root sits deeper, lodged in the internal posture a person carries long before the first toxic incident ever unfolds.

At its core, toxic behavior is fueled by an attitude of superiority, entitlement, or emotional domination. It's the belief—whether conscious or subconscious—that my needs matter more than yours, my control is necessary, or my emotions have the right to rule this relationship. This mindset takes many forms, often shaped long before adulthood: environments where someone had power but lacked compassion, where they were taught that domination equals love, or where they learned that vulnerability is dangerous and control is survival. **When control becomes the strategy, threat becomes the language of the relationship.**

This attitude shows up in subtle ways at first. A dismissive tone. A refusal to take accountability. A pattern of shifting blame. Eventually, it grows into more overt behaviors: manipulation, humiliation, threats, emotional withdrawal, or physical intimidation. The behavior escalates, but the underlying message stays the same: I get to decide how this relationship works. I get to set the rules. Your comfort, safety, and boundaries are negotiable. Mine are not.

What makes toxic attitudes so damaging is that they're self-reinforcing. A toxic person often sees their partner's fear, their coworker's silence, or their child's compliance as confirmation that their attitude is justified. "See? This is why I must lead like this. This is why I act this way." The relationship becomes a stage where their emotional instability masquerades as authority.

And while toxic behavior is often rooted in trauma or past wounds, that origin does not excuse the harm it causes. It simply explains how the attitude formed. Someone who grew up in chaos may normalize chaos. Someone who never had control may cling to it obsessively. Someone who was abandoned may weaponize fear to keep others close. But no amount of pain justifies inflicting pain on others.

The most dangerous part of toxic behavior is how slowly it rewires the relationship. The victim begins questioning their own reality. They begin believing they're the cause of the problem. They start adjusting themselves to "keep the peace." That shift is exactly what the toxic attitude feeds on—silence, compliance, fear, and self-blame. **And over time, the nervous system learns: safety depends on shrinking.**

Here's the truth: *Toxic behavior doesn't simply break relationships. It breaks people. And it always begins with the attitude beneath the surface.*

Until that attitude is confronted, acknowledged, and transformed, the behavior will not stop. Changing actions without addressing beliefs is like putting a bandage on a wound that needs surgery—the deeper issue remains untouched.

The attitude at the root of toxic behavior says:
"I am right. I am owed. I must be in control. Your feelings are secondary. Your boundaries are optional." And this attitude turns every interaction into a power struggle rather than a partnership.

Understanding this root is the first step toward healing and safety. It gives language to what victims often feel but cannot articulate. It shifts the focus from blaming yourself to recognizing the truth:
You didn't cause their attitude—and you cannot fix it alone.

Toxic Behavior & Assumptions: *Distorted Justifications for Harm*

Toxic behavior rarely stands on its own—it leans heavily on assumptions that twist reality, justify harmful actions, and silence accountability. These assumptions are like smoke that blinds both the abuser and the victim, creating a version of the relationship that feels impossible to challenge or escape.

One of the most dangerous assumptions is "They made me act this way." This mindset shifts the blame off the person who caused harm and onto the person who experienced it. Instead of taking responsibility, the toxic individual convinces themselves—and sometimes the victim—that the victim's reactions, questions, boundaries, or emotions are the reason for their outburst. This assumption becomes a weapon. It reframes abuse as a "reaction," when in reality, it's a choice.

Another corrosive assumption is “This is just how relationships work.” When someone grows up in chaos, control, violence, or emotional instability, they may see dysfunction as normal. Toxic behavior becomes part of the script they learned early in life. Instead of questioning the behavior, they accept it as the expected rhythm of connection. This assumption traps both parties in a cycle where harm is predictable but never challenged, because neither person believes they are allowed to want—or expect—better.

Then there is the deeply manipulative belief: “If they really cared, they’d put up with it.” This assumption turns love into an endurance test. It treats patience as permission, and devotion as a reason to tolerate pain. It teaches the victim that boundaries equal betrayal and silence equals loyalty. This mindset is particularly dangerous because it flips the relationship upside down: the more someone loves, the more they tolerate; the more they tolerate, the more the toxic behavior grows. What looks like endurance becomes entrapment.

These assumptions do not just distort truth—they rewrite it. They create a narrative where the toxic person becomes the misunderstood victim, and the true victim becomes the one responsible for maintaining the peace. Over time, the person on the receiving end begins to question their own reality:
“Maybe I did push too hard.”
“Maybe this is normal.”
“Maybe I’m overreacting.”
“Maybe this is what love looks like.”

This is how assumptions sustain toxicity: by making the intolerable seem tolerable, the unacceptable seem inevitable, and the harmful seem justified. **And when the nervous system is already living in fear, those distortions become easier to believe.**

But here's the truth beneath the illusion: Toxic behavior is never justified. Mistreatment is never a valid response. And love is never proven through suffering.

Assumptions may prop up toxic behavior for a while, but once those assumptions are exposed and challenged, the cycle begins to crack. And that shift—naming the lie—is the first breath of freedom for anyone tangled in a toxic dynamic.

Toxic Behavior & Expectations: *When Control Disguises Itself as "Standards"*

Toxic behavior is often held in place by distorted expectations—demands that go far beyond what is healthy, fair, or even human. These expectations create relationship dynamics where one person's comfort becomes the priority and everyone else is expected to shrink, adjust, or suffer to maintain it. When expectations become rigid, unrealistic, and rooted in control, they turn relationships into pressure cookers of dysfunction.

In romantic relationships, toxic expectations often take the form of emotional domination. A partner may expect the other to be emotionally bulletproof—never upset, never triggered, never needing reassurance. Or they may expect obedience, availability on demand, or immediate compliance with their moods and needs. The unspoken message becomes: "Your emotions are optional. Mine are mandatory."

In friendships, toxic expectations show up as suffocating loyalty. Instead of mutual support, the relationship becomes a one-way loyalty contract. A toxic friend may expect you to choose them over your own well-being, to silence your boundaries, or to absorb emotional burdens they have no intention of addressing themselves. Their expectation of loyalty stretches so far that it begins to tear at your mental and emotional stability.

In the workplace, toxic expectations are often cloaked as "strong leadership" or "high standards." Employees are expected to tolerate verbal aggression, unrealistic workloads, public criticism, or emotional volatility—all in the name of productivity. Toxic managers often believe their pressure is motivational, when it is in fact manipulative. Instead of leadership, it becomes tyranny with a professional title.

Across all relationship types, these expectations demand one thing: the suppression of others' needs to maintain the comfort, ego, or control of the toxic individual. And that is not love. It is not loyalty. It is not respect.

It is control—plain and simple.

When someone expects you to mute your pain, ignore your instincts, or minimize your humanity so they can feel more powerful, their expectation becomes a tool of domination. And when you repeatedly adjust yourself to meet those expectations, the toxic dynamic strengthens. You begin carrying the weight of their emotional world while they carry none of yours. **This is how survival replaces connection—slowly, then suddenly.**

The harsh reality is this: Toxic expectations do not ask for cooperation—they demand compliance. They don't build connection—they suffocate it. They don't foster love—they distort it into something unrecognizable.

Healthy relationships—whether romantic, familial, or professional—thrive on mutual expectations that honor both people, not one. They allow breathing room, individuality, and shared responsibility. Toxic expectations do the opposite: they confine, restrict, and control.

Naming these expectations is the first step toward breaking their power. Because once you recognize that someone is expecting you to shrink so they can feel big, you reclaim the right to stand fully in your truth, your needs, and your boundaries.

Breaking the Cycle:
Choosing Healing Over Harm

Toxic behaviors do not dissolve with time, apologies, or wishful thinking. They don't disappear because someone "didn't mean it," or because both people hope things will get better. Toxicity ends only when it is interrupted—when someone finally decides that the cycle stops here. Breaking the cycle requires courage, clarity, and a radical shift in the internal compass that has been steering the relationship off course.

The first step is reforming the attitude at the root of the behavior. Control, manipulation, intimidation, or emotional harm are not expressions of love, leadership, passion, or "just how I am." They are warning signs—signals that something within the relationship is deeply misaligned. Reframing the attitude means recognizing that love is not proven through fear, compliance, or silence. It is proven through safety, respect, and emotional responsibility. When someone shifts their internal posture from "I need control" to "I need connection," everything changes.

Next comes challenging the assumptions that have been used to justify the harm. No one deserves to be mistreated. Not because they "pushed the wrong button." Not because they "always say the wrong thing." Not because they "know how I get." Abuse—emotional, physical, psychological, or verbal—is never an understandable reaction. It is never earned. It is never deserved. Healthy relationships are designed to build, not break; to empower, not diminish; to protect, not expose. Challenging assumptions means naming the lies:

"This is normal."
"They made me act this way."
"Real love is supposed to hurt sometimes."

These beliefs must be uprooted for healing to begin.

And then there is redefining expectations—the quiet, powerful recalibration that shifts the entire relational dynamic. Healthy expectations honor boundaries, not bulldoze them. They recognize equality, not hierarchy. They value emotional safety, not emotional dominance. In a healthy relationship, the expectation is mutual: both people grow, both people feel safe, both people have a voice. Redefining expectations doesn't just change how you treat others—it changes what you allow, tolerate, and accept.

Breaking the cycle also requires accountability—not the kind that comes with forced apologies or temporary behavior changes, but the kind that acknowledges harm, seeks support, and commits to transformation. Abuse cannot be healed with excuses. Toxic patterns cannot be repaired with promises. Change begins the moment someone says, "I was wrong—and I'm willing to do the work."

But breaking the cycle is not only for the person causing harm. It is also for the person experiencing it. Naming the toxicity, reclaiming your voice, setting boundaries, seeking support, standing firm in your worth—these are not acts of rebellion. They are acts of self-respect. Sometimes breaking the cycle means repairing the relationship. Other times, it means protecting yourself from it.

The truth is simple but powerful: Toxic behavior destroys connection—but healing becomes possible the moment honesty enters the room. When we choose respect over control, accountability over excuses, and truth over denial, the cycle that once felt unbreakable begins to loosen, weaken, and finally fall apart.

Breaking the cycle doesn't promise an easy path. It promises a free one. And on the other side of that freedom are relationships built on clarity, safety, mutual honor, and real love—the kind that doesn't harm, the kind that never has to be survived.

Reflection Activity

Let's pause and face the truth: I'm talking to both survivors and those who've caused harm. That might feel uncomfortable—but healing doesn't happen without honesty.

Many people are trapped in toxic relationships without fully realizing it. A study from the National Institutes of Health reports that nearly 50% of Americans have experienced emotional abuse from a partner. Another from Kolmac Integrated Behavioral Health Centers found that 84% of women and 75% of men have endured toxic friendships. That's not rare—it's a cultural crisis.

This conversation is hard. But some people are silently begging for help—not through words, but through behaviors: withdrawal, anxiety, numbness, anger. Toxicity wears many masks, and some are so subtle we don't notice until it's too late.

Before I go any further, I need to say this with urgency and compassion: If you are experiencing physical abuse, it is never acceptable.

Help is available.

- National Domestic Violence Hotline: 1-800-799-7233 (SAFE)
- Text "START" to 88788
- Visit thehotline.org (Live chat available)

I understand how hard it can be to seek help. I've been there. I've lived through more than one abusive relationship and—like many—never used those resources. But I did call 911… after jumping off a second-story balcony to escape physical abuse. I know what it's like to fear leaving—and to fear staying.

My empathy doesn't stop with the victim. It stretches—boldly and controversially—to the assailant. Why? Because no one wakes up and just decides to become abusive. Pain has a history. And while nothing excuses harming others, understanding the roots is essential to breaking the cycle. "Hurt people, hurt people" is more than a saying—it's a map of generational trauma.

Let's be clear:
• The victim might believe, "I can't leave. They love me." But love isn't the question—safety is.
• The assailant might believe, "This is just how relationships are." But just because it's familiar doesn't mean it's right.

And abuse isn't always romantic. Maybe your workplace feels emotionally draining. Maybe family gatherings are filled with tension and disrespect. Maybe you've tolerated toxic friendships because you didn't have the words to name them. Now you do.

If you're constantly feeling small, controlled, guilty, or like you're losing yourself—stop. Ask yourself: Is this relationship healthy, or is it toxic?

A New Beginning
The first step to healing is naming the problem—and being brave enough to address it. You don't need to burn every bridge. Sometimes, healing means repairing. Other times, it means walking away. But it always begins with new attitudes and new expectations.

So, here's your challenge: **Activity:**
Think of a place or relationship that drains you. Maybe it's your job. Maybe it's someone close. What toxicity lingers in that space? What assumptions have allowed it to fester? And what small action can you take to shift the culture?

Let's become people who speak life into spaces once ruled by silence. Who stop cycles by calling things by name. Who know that empathy can hold both accountability and hope. Take a moment to process your thoughts, reflect, and begin your healing journey:

Healing is possible—for all of us.

3H. Lack of Boundaries

Healthy relationships—whether romantic, professional, familial, or within a community—depend on clear, honored, and consistently respected boundaries. Boundaries are not walls; they are guidelines that define where one person ends and another begins. They protect our emotional well-being, preserve our identity, and create space for genuine, sustainable connection. Without them, relationships begin to suffocate under the weight of constant intrusion, unrealistic demands, or emotional overexposure.

A lack of boundaries doesn't always begin with harmful intentions. In fact, it often begins during the "honeymoon" stage of any new relationship or environment. The excitement of newness makes being present, helpful, involved, or inseparable feel natural—even energizing.

In a new job, you might spend late nights in the office, fueled by purpose and momentum. In a new romance, you may want to absorb every moment of closeness. In a new ministry or volunteer role, you show up early, stay late, and pour yourself into every service.

During those early stages, the lines blur because the energy is high. But when the honeymoon fades and your normal rhythm returns, taking a step back can feel like a betrayal—to others and sometimes even to yourself. You suddenly feel pressure to maintain the pace you set, and the people around you expect you to continue operating as you did in the beginning. What makes this dynamic even more complicated is that often, the boundary wasn't crossed—it was never established to begin with.

So how do we recover from a lack of boundaries?
How do we rebuild when the pace we created is no longer sustainable?

First, we must understand that it is not the lack of boundaries alone that destroys relationships—it's the three silent relationship destroyers beneath it: attitude, assumptions, and expectations. Boundaries crumble when one person assumes access, expects availability, or carries an attitude that disregards the needs and limits of others. Boundaries also collapse when we expect ourselves to over-function or when we assume others automatically "get" what we need without ever stating it. **And when boundaries stay unclear, the nervous system often shifts into survival—over-functioning, shutting down, or people-pleasing just to keep the peace.**

Understanding this helps us navigate the repair.

Lack of Boundaries and Expectations: *The Core of Boundary Issues*

At its core, boundary problems are rooted in unrealistic, unclear, or unspoken expectations—of ourselves or of others. When expectations around personal space, emotional capacity, privacy, or responsibilities are poorly defined, relationships become strained, imbalanced, and emotionally draining.

Sometimes the expectation is inward:
We expect ourselves to always show up, always serve, always be available, and always say yes—even when it costs us our peace or health. Overextending ourselves becomes normalized, and rest feels like guilt instead of self-preservation. **In this space, "yes" becomes a reflex—not because you want to, but because your body has learned that saying no might not feel safe.**

Other times, the expectation is outward: We unintentionally place friends, partners, coworkers, or even leaders in roles they were never meant to fill. We expect one person to meet all of our emotional needs, unintentionally creating codependency. Or we expect others to tolerate our overstepping—believing they should understand our stress, our intentions, or our history without requiring accountability or adjustment.

And often, boundaries break down in environments where roles blur. A partner becomes your therapist. A boss becomes your regulator. A friend becomes your emotional dumping ground. A church becomes your whole identity. When the roles blur, expectations blur—and someone always ends up carrying emotional weight they were never built to hold.

When boundaries are not clearly stated, communicated, or respected, frustration starts simmering under the surface. Resentment quietly grows. Emotional exhaustion sets in. Even the most loving relationship can begin to feel claustrophobic, heavy, or one-sided. And instead of identifying the real issue—unclear or violated boundaries—people often mislabel the fallout as incompatibility, lack of love, or failure.

But the truth is simple: Boundaries don't destroy relationships—ignoring them does.

And ignoring them happens when expectations go unchallenged.

Lack of Boundaries and Attitude: *A Mindset That Undervalues Boundaries*

A lack of boundaries rarely begins with behavior—it begins with a mindset. How a person views personal autonomy, emotional space, and the right to say "no" determines whether they honor boundaries or bulldoze through them. Attitude sets the tone: if someone believes boundaries are optional, unnecessary, or threatening, they will either struggle to set them or routinely ignore the boundaries of others.

One of the most common attitudes behind boundary issues is the people-pleasing mentality. This mindset treats boundaries as acts of selfishness rather than self-respect. People who carry this attitude often equate saying "no" with disappointing others, losing approval, or risking rejection. They overextend themselves emotionally, physically, and mentally because the fear of letting someone down is stronger than the need for personal well-being. Their attitude whispers, "If I protect myself, someone else will suffer." But in reality, the suffering grows when their internal limits are never honored. **For many, this isn't just preference—it's conditioning. A nervous system trained to avoid conflict will often choose over-giving as protection.**

On the opposite end of the spectrum is the control-oriented mindset—a posture that sees boundaries as obstacles rather than protections. Someone with this mindset may resist limits because they believe that keeping unrestricted access to others maintains their influence, power, or emotional dominance. Boundaries feel like rejection or rebellion instead of healthy self-differentiation. They may interpret someone's "I need space" as an insult, a threat, or a challenge. Their attitude frames boundaries not as a tool for connection, but as something to override or bypass.

And then there is the complicated dynamic of emotional entanglement, where someone equates constant closeness with love, loyalty, or stability. This mindset romanticizes enmeshment and interprets distance—or even healthy independence—as abandonment. Instead of seeing boundaries as a way to preserve emotional health, they interpret them as barriers that reduce connection. Their attitude insists, "If we care about each other, we shouldn't need space." But this is a flawed belief, because connection without boundaries becomes suffocation, not intimacy. **True safety includes breathing room.**

When a person's attitude undervalues boundaries, relationships become uneven and unbalanced. Either the person collapses their own needs to keep peace, or they erode the needs of others to maintain control. In either case, the result is the same: resentment grows, exhaustion follows, and the relationship slowly begins to fracture under pressure.

Boundaries do not fail because they are unnecessary—they fail because the attitude behind them was never strong enough to support them in the first place.

Lack of Boundaries and Assumptions:
Misguided Beliefs That Sabotage Connection

Boundary violations often stem not from intentional harm, but from misguided assumptions—stories people create in their minds about what boundaries mean, how they work, and how others will react to them. These assumptions act like faulty maps, guiding people in the wrong direction while convincing them they're doing the right thing.

One harmful assumption is the belief that "If they cared, they'd know what I need." This assumption places the responsibility for emotional clarity on others, expecting them to read minds or interpret signals that were never clearly communicated. When someone holds this assumption, they may feel deeply hurt when their needs aren't met—yet they never verbalized those needs in the first place. The boundary wasn't crossed; it was never expressed.

Another destructive assumption is "If I set a boundary, they'll leave." This belief creates fear around self-protection. People who carry this assumption see limits not as healthy guidelines but as threats to the relationship itself. They believe that saying "no," requesting space, or asserting their needs will push people away. As a result, they tolerate disrespect, absorb emotional burdens, and allow others to overstep simply to avoid the fear of abandonment. But this assumption keeps the relationship unstable, because it builds connection on sacrifice rather than honesty. **And when abandonment has been a real wound, the body treats boundaries like danger—even when the mind knows they're healthy.**

The third common belief is "Boundaries mean shutting people out." This assumption confuses protection with isolation. It frames boundaries as walls rather than bridges, as rejection rather than self-respect. When someone believes this, they avoid setting boundaries because they fear creating distance or hurting someone's feelings. Yet healthy boundaries do the opposite—they preserve connection by preventing burnout, resentment, and emotional suffocation.

These false assumptions create a relational landscape where no one truly knows where the limits are—or worse, where the limits exist but no one feels safe enough to name them. As a result, people end up tolerating behaviors that drain them or placing expectations on others that they never agreed to fulfill.

Boundaries are not weapons. They are not punishments. They are not walls. They are instructions for how to love you well—and how you will love others well in return.

When we challenge the assumptions that distort the purpose of boundaries, we give ourselves permission to create relationships built on respect, clarity, and emotional balance. Only then can boundaries become what they were always meant to be: tools of protection, not division; clarity, not conflict; connection, not distance.

Breaking the Cycle: *Restoring Boundaries with Confidence and Clarity*

Breaking the cycle of unhealthy or nonexistent boundaries does not happen by accident—it happens by intention. Boundaries do not suddenly appear because we wish for them. They emerge when we decide that our well-being, identity, and emotional safety are worth protecting. Restoring boundaries requires courage, clarity, and a shift in the three relationship dynamics that shape every stressor: attitude, assumptions, and expectations.

The first step is redefining your attitude toward boundaries. Many people carry the belief that boundaries are selfish, rude, or unloving. But that mindset is exactly what keeps people trapped in cycles of burnout, resentment, and emotional depletion. Shifting your attitude means embracing a new truth: boundaries are an expression of self-respect, not self-centeredness. They protect you so you can show up in relationships—not drained, not resentful, but whole. When you shift from "I owe everyone my constant availability" to "I owe myself the right to rest and breathe," you reclaim the emotional space needed for healthy connection. **And you teach your nervous system that clarity can coexist with safety.**

Next comes challenging the assumptions that make boundaries feel dangerous. The belief that "people will leave if I speak up" forces you to sacrifice authenticity for acceptance. The belief that "they should just know what I need" sets both sides up for disappointment. And the belief that "boundaries push people away" ignores the truth that lack of boundaries pushes them away faster. To break the cycle, you must dismantle the stories that have kept you silent. Boundaries do not ruin healthy relationships—they reveal them. Anyone who is meant to grow with you will respect your limits. Anyone who doesn't was benefiting from your lack of them.

Then comes resetting expectations—for yourself and others. Boundaries require you to release the expectation that you must be everything to everyone. That you must always say yes. That your worth is measured by how much you give, fix, or absorb. It also requires you to set new expectations for the people in your life: that your time matters, your needs matter, your voice matters, and your limits matter. Healthy relationships honor these expectations. Toxic ones resist them. And that clarity, while sometimes painful, becomes freeing.

Breaking the cycle also requires practice. Boundaries are not one-time statements—they are ongoing commitments. You will feel discomfort. You will feel guilt. You may even feel fear. But discomfort does not mean you're doing something wrong—it means you're doing something new. Every time you choose clarity over silence, every time you say "I can't do that today," every time you protect your emotional space, you reinforce a new pattern of self-respect.

Most importantly, restoring boundaries brings the relationship back into balance. When your limits are respected, you no longer have to carry more than your share. You no longer shrink, overextend, or apologize for having needs. You make room for reciprocity. You make room for real connection. You make room for peace.

The cycle breaks the moment you decide you are worthy of healthy limits. It stabilizes when you communicate those limits clearly. It solidifies when you enforce them consistently.

And as you grow stronger in your boundaries, your relationships grow healthier—because they're built on truth, not obligation; mutual respect, not imbalance; clarity, not confusion.

Healthy boundaries don't push people away. They allow the right people to come close.

Reflection Activity

If you're anything like me—someone who loves to "be there" for others, to support and help, to be selfless—you might struggle with creating healthy boundaries. I know I did for most of my adult life. I was the person everyone could count on, no matter the situation. But this came at a cost. I overextended myself, and I didn't realize how deep the toll was until I hit a wall. I was exhausted, my health was failing, and my mind was spent. It all came down to one thing: I failed to establish boundaries for myself.

I had to face the hard truth: I was allowing others' expectations to dictate my energy, my time, and my well-being. Everyone knew that if they called on me, I'd be there. It didn't matter that I had a full-time job, personal commitments, or that I was drained. But I quickly learned that this lack of boundaries was a recipe for burnout. I needed to adjust the expectations I allowed to form around me and make room for my own needs.

A big part of this was adjusting my attitude. I had to realize that I could only love and care for others from a place of overflow. If my cup was empty, how could I possibly pour into someone else's? The truth is, if I wasn't caring for myself first, I was doing no one any favors, especially not those I loved. My attitude shifted when I understood that taking care of myself wasn't selfish—it was necessary.

I also had to challenge some of my assumptions. I'd assumed that my loved ones would be upset if I took a step back. But in reality, they recognized it. They could see I needed space to rest and recharge. The people who truly cared about me understood that boundaries were a sign of strength, not weakness. Setting boundaries didn't mean I was abandoning anyone; it meant I was protecting my well-being so I could show up as the best version of myself. **And as I practiced, my nervous system stopped treating "no" like danger and started treating it like wisdom.**

This isn't just about family or friends, though. The lack of boundaries can affect every area of your life—especially your professional life. When we don't establish clear boundaries at work, we can burn out, feel resentment toward colleagues, and create a toxic environment. It's no different from what we've discussed before. Without boundaries, toxic dynamics can easily creep in, whether at home or in the workplace.

So, I want to ask you: In what area of your life are you absolutely exhausted and in need of boundaries? Where are you overextending yourself to the point that it's draining you? Go ahead and reflect on that right now. I give you permission—pause everything and think about yourself. This moment of self-awareness is a step toward healing and growth. Don't wait until you hit a wall. Take a moment to think about what you need and what boundaries will help you reclaim your energy and well-being.

Take a deep breath. You deserve this.

31. Trauma or Past Experiences:

The emotional baggage we carry from past relationships or life experiences can deeply affect our ability to build healthy, trusting connections. When trauma remains unresolved, it shows up in ways we don't always recognize—defensive walls, a quick retreat when things feel uncomfortable, trust issues, or patterns of self-sabotage. These lingering wounds don't stay in the past; they leak into the present, hurting us and sometimes unintentionally hurting the people we care about.

One of the challenges with trauma is that it often **lies dormant until something triggers it**. A tone of voice, a misunderstanding, a moment of disappointment—suddenly the old pain resurfaces, and we react not to the current situation but to the weight of what came before. And when trauma is intersectional, the vulnerability becomes even more complex. Intersectional trauma forms when multiple layers of harm—oppression, discrimination, cultural experiences, and personal history—interact and collide. It is not a single wound but a network of wounds that shape how a person moves through the world, how they interpret relationships, and how they experience safety, stress, and healing.

When we bring trauma into our relationships, we aren't consciously trying to involve others in our past pain. We don't set out to project old wounds onto the people we love or work beside. Yet the burden of past trauma can create significant stress, making connections harder and communication more fragile. Still, we must be clear: trauma itself is not what destroys the relationship.

Trauma influences how we respond, not who we are.
It shapes our inner landscape—and often our reflexes—but it doesn't predetermine the outcome.

In **the AAE Framework™,** trauma and past experiences most closely align with assumptions, because they filter how we interpret current situations through the lens of past hurt. But trauma also impacts our attitude, influencing how open or guarded we become, and our expectations, shaping what we believe is possible for us in relationships—whether we expect disappointment, abandonment, connection, or safety.

Understanding the influence of trauma doesn't excuse harmful behavior, but it does illuminate the path toward healing. Awareness allows us to separate the past from the present and choose responses that support growth rather than repeat old cycles.

Trauma and Past Experiences & Assumptions: *The Lens of Past Pain*

Trauma and past experiences do more than linger in memory—they reshape the way we interpret the world. They create powerful, often subconscious assumptions about how relationships work, and these assumptions become the lens through which we view every interaction. Instead of seeing people as they are, we see them through the shadows of what we've endured. As a result, our behaviors can become defensive, guarded, or avoidant long before we realize why.

These assumptions don't come from nowhere; they are born from survival. When pain is repeated, the mind learns to anticipate it. When trust is broken, the heart learns to protect itself. And when the nervous system has learned danger, it can misread neutral moments as threats. But without awareness, these protective strategies turn inward and begin sabotaging the very connections we long for.

Common trauma-driven assumptions sound like:
• "People always leave." → This assumption expects

abandonment as a guarantee. It creates either emotional detachment to avoid hurt or clinginess to prevent loss.

• "Love means pain." → This assumption associates closeness with suffering, making intimacy feel dangerous or temporary.

• "No one can be trusted." → This assumption anticipates betrayal, making it difficult—sometimes impossible—to form secure bonds.

• "If I open up, I'll be judged or rejected." → This assumption frames vulnerability as a risk, building emotional walls that keep people at a distance.

These beliefs operate below the surface, shaping reactions before logic even enters the room. They create patterns of fear, withdrawal, hypervigilance, or self-sabotage—patterns that feel like protection but ultimately reinforce the very pain we're trying to avoid.

When trauma shapes assumptions, relationships become filtered through past wounds instead of present realities. The goal is not to blame ourselves for these responses, but to recognize them, challenge them, and begin healing the lens through which we see connection.

Trauma and Past Experiences & Attitude:
A Mindset Shaped by the Past

Trauma doesn't just influence how we interpret relationships—it also shapes the attitude we bring into them. Our posture toward connection, trust, vulnerability, and closeness is often built on what we've survived. When past experiences have been painful, unfair, or unsafe, the mind adopts attitudes that seem protective in the moment but become harmful over time. These attitudes don't form because someone is "difficult" or unwilling to connect; they form because the past taught them that connection comes with a cost.

Common trauma-shaped attitudes include:

• **Defensive Attitude**: A mindset of "hurt them before they hurt me." This attitude develops as a **shield**, preventing vulnerability by striking first—emotionally, verbally, or through withdrawal.

• **Hyper-Independence**: The belief that relying on others is dangerous, and that total self-reliance is the only way to avoid disappointment or betrayal. It masquerades as strength but often comes from deep fear.

• **Low Self-Worth**: A quiet, painful belief that one is undeserving of love, respect, or kindness. This attitude can lead people to tolerate toxic dynamics or minimize their own needs, simply because they don't believe they deserve better.

These attitudes were born as survival mechanisms—responses that once helped someone navigate trauma. But over time, they become barriers that block healthy connection. They can prevent people from believing that safe, fulfilling, trusting relationships are even possible. Healing begins when we recognize that these attitudes are not reflections of who we are—they are reflections of what we lived through. And with awareness, they can be reshaped.

Trauma and Past Experiences & Expectations:
Carrying the Past into the Present

Trauma doesn't stay neatly tucked away in memory—it shapes what we expect from relationships long before they even begin. When someone has lived through hurt, abandonment, chaos, or instability, those experiences create internal forecasts about how relationships will unfold. These expectations become the script the mind prepares for, often without permission. And unless we examine them, they repeat the past in the present.

Common trauma-shaped expectations include:
• **Expecting Rejection**: Anticipating that others will eventually withdraw, lose interest, or betray trust. This expectation creates emotional distance before a relationship even has the chance to grow.
• **Expecting Conflict**: Believing that relationships inevitably involve tension, drama, or control. When conflict is familiar—especially from childhood—it can become the default expectation, even when peace is possible.
• **Expecting Conditional** Love: Believing that affection, respect, or attention must be earned through sacrifice, over-functioning, or people-pleasing. This expectation often forms when someone learned that love was tied to performance rather than belonging.

When trauma dictates expectations, people can find themselves repeating old relational patterns without realizing it. They may push others away to avoid pain, tolerate harmful dynamics because they feel familiar, or struggle to recognize healthy love and support when it is offered. These expectations are not chosen—they are inherited from experiences that taught the nervous system to prepare for disappointment.

Healing begins with naming these expectations, challenging where they came from, and learning to rewrite the script so the past no longer dictates the future.

Breaking the Cycle

Because trauma and past experiences shape our assumptions, attitude, and expectations, breaking the cycle requires intentional, courageous work. Healing doesn't happen by accident—it happens through conscious choices that interrupt old patterns and create space for something new.

• **Challenging Assumptions**: Healing begins with questioning the internal stories formed by past pain. Instead of automatically expecting abandonment, betrayal, or disappointment, we learn to ask, "Is this truth, or is this trauma speaking?" This shift creates room for present-day relationships to be seen for what they truly are—not filtered through old wounds.

• **Shifting Attitude**: Trauma often shapes a defensive or fearful posture toward connection. Breaking the cycle means slowly cultivating a mindset rooted in openness, self-worth, and trust—especially in relationships that have proven safe. This doesn't mean ignoring red flags; it means not allowing fear to lead every interaction.

• **Reevaluating Expectations**: When expectations come from past hurt, they set us up to relive the same patterns again and again. Healing involves redefining what is possible—allowing for balanced, reciprocal relationships instead of reenacting old dynamics. It means expecting respect, expecting communication, and expecting emotional safety, not because you've "earned" it but because you deserve it.

Trauma may explain how certain patterns formed, but it does not have to define how they continue. With self-awareness, intentional healing, and the willingness to rewrite old narratives, we can build relationships grounded in trust, security, and genuine connection. The past shaped the lens—but you have the power to reshape the vision.

Reflection Activity

If you've read my previous book, *I Wish Someone Would Have Told Me That*, you know that I've experienced enough trauma to earn an honorary degree in it. That trauma shaped who I was and how I showed up in relationships. On one hand, it built resilience in me—I knew how to persevere, no matter what. But on the other hand, it came with a heavy load. Being molested as a child, abandoned, becoming a teenage mother, enduring physically abusive relationships—it was a lot of baggage to carry. I trusted no one. I needed no one. My attitude toward protecting my heart was rigid. I was out of there before anyone trampled too hard on my heart. I suffered terribly from what I now recognize as flight syndrome.

I knew I had flight syndrome, but sometimes I didn't fully understand it. What I didn't realize then was that it was caused by my trauma and my attitude toward it. The way I reacted to the pain, the betrayal, and the loss—wasn't just a survival instinct. It was my way of avoiding facing the pain I didn't know how to heal from.

And this approach, though protective, was also a relationship destroyer.

It prevented me from developing and maintaining real, healthy connections with others. Trauma has a way of making us push people away, whether we intend to or not. If we hold on to our past wounds, they become a wall we erect between ourselves and others, keeping love and trust at arm's length.

At the same time, I was desperately yearning for love. I remember thinking, over and over again, "I just want someone to love me, like I love others." I prayed for it—constantly. But you want to know how I finally let go of my past and started living a present life free from the anchor of the past? I realized something that I should have known long ago: I am not my past experiences. Yes, I learned from them, but they do not define me. I can let them go. I can leave them behind, because they no longer need to show up and try to "protect" me.

In fact, they were doing just the opposite—keeping me stuck and preventing me from building new, healthy relationships.

But trauma doesn't just stay in the personal realm. It seeps into other areas of our lives too, including the workplace. When we don't address our trauma, it can manifest in our professional relationships and environments. Have you ever seen anyone experience emotional outbursts when faced with stress or other triggers, or maybe you've personally distanced yourself from colleagues who are trying to get to know you because you were afraid of building that connection. Perhaps, like me, you've had moments of deep distrust, which made it hard to navigate different relationships at work. Undealt-with trauma can create a constant sense of tension, defensiveness, or withdrawal—making it difficult to thrive in work settings, or even to build supportive professional relationships. These patterns can ultimately hold us back from career growth and creating healthy, collaborative environments. Trauma is a relationship destructive force, not just at home but also at work.

There's a scripture from the Bible that says,

"This is the day the Lord has made; let us rejoice and be glad in it." (Psalm 118:24).

This has become my life's anthem. It's a reminder that, even in the face of hardship, each new day is a gift. And the beauty of it is that my new positive anthem has more verses—verses about new mercies from God every single day. I can hit the reset button every day if I need to, making sure that eventually I would leave the past where it belongs—behind me.

The bottom line is, how can you fully enjoy today if you're still living in the past? How can you truly embrace the gift of this day if you assume everyone is out to get you? That shift in my mindset—the choice to live in the present instead of the past—was one of the healthiest decisions I've ever made. So now, when I meet people, they get the Dr.

Kay of today, not the one from yesterday or the one that might be living in the future.

Now I want to ask you: Do you need to let go of your past trauma? Is it creeping into all of your relationships—personal and professional? Is it showing up in your workplace and impacting how you engage with colleagues, supervisors, or clients? Guess what—it's in the past. I challenge you to leave it there. Don't let it keep holding you back from being fully present, in both your personal and professional life. Don't let it keep you from experiencing the fullness of love, connection, and success that you deserve. I'm not even going to ask you to write this one down. In fact, I'm going to suggest the opposite. Instead of focusing on what's behind you, take a moment to write down how you are going to enjoy today. Right now. This moment. How will you embrace the present and make the most of this day?

I encourage you to take a deep breath, let go of the baggage, and commit to living in the beauty of today. You've got this.

3J External Stressors:

Life is full of stress—raising families, managing commitments, navigating financial strain, balancing work demands, coping with health concerns, and living under the weight of societal expectations. When these pressures build, our emotional bandwidth shrinks. We become more irritable, easily overwhelmed, withdrawn, or less attentive to the people around us—not because they've done anything wrong, but because our internal resources are stretched thin.

External stress erodes the emotional energy required to maintain meaningful connections. It weakens relationships at the exact moments when they need the most nurturing. And unlike internal stressors, these outside pressures cannot simply be ignored. Bills must be paid. Children must be cared for. Doctors' appointments must be kept. Deadlines must be met. Responsibilities march on whether our hearts feel ready or not.

Some people respond to this pressure by reducing the number of relationships or commitments in their lives. They may choose to stay single to avoid emotional overload, decline extra responsibilities at work, or limit social interactions to preserve a sense of peace. And these choices are completely understandable—sometimes essential for survival. Yet even in those protective decisions, something inside of us still longs for connection. As humans, we are wired for relationships, even when life convinces us we don't have the **capacity** for one.

External stressors primarily align with attitude, because they shape how we respond to pressure—whether we become defensive, distant, short-tempered, or emotionally numb. But these stressors also bleed into our expectations and assumptions. Under pressure, we may expect others to "just understand," assume they should anticipate our needs, or believe they are failing us when they don't offer support in the exact way we imagined. Stress distorts how we perceive responsibility, support, commitment, and resilience.

The goal is not to eliminate stress—that's impossible. The goal is to recognize how outside pressures influence the way we show up in our relationships and to choose responses that create connection rather than deepen disconnection. When we acknowledge the weight we're carrying, we make room for compassion—both for ourselves and for those walking alongside us.

External Stressors and Attitude: *How We Respond to Stress*

External stressors—financial strain, work demands, health challenges, or societal pressures—are an unavoidable part of life. We cannot always choose what happens to us, but we can choose the attitude we bring to those moments. That attitude becomes the defining factor in whether stress strengthens our relationships or silently fractures them.

Different attitudes emerge when stress takes hold:

- **Resilient Attitude**: Seeing challenges as opportunities for growth, collaboration, and problem-solving. This mindset invites teamwork and reinforces connection during difficult seasons.
- **Defensive Attitude**: Directing frustration toward others, becoming short-tempered, or emotionally shutting down. This attitude often blames the nearest person, even if they had no part in causing the stress.
- **Victim Mentality**: Feeling powerless and expecting others to carry emotional weight or fix circumstances without contributing to the solution. This creates imbalance and resentment in relationships.
- **Avoidant Attitude**: Pretending stress isn't there, ignoring issues that need attention, or pushing problems aside until

they become bigger. This avoidance breeds tension, distance, and unspoken frustration.

When stress fuels a negative attitude, it doesn't just create conflict—it creates emotional disconnection. The relationship begins to feel strained, unpredictable, or unsafe, not because love or commitment has changed, but because stress has distorted the way we show up.

Recognizing this pattern allows us to shift from reacting to stress to responding with intention. And that shift can make the difference between relationships that crumble under pressure and relationships that grow through it.

External Stressors and Expectations:
What We Believe Others Should Do During Stress

Stress doesn't just drain our energy—it reshapes what we expect from the people around us. When life becomes overwhelming, expectations can quietly shift into unrealistic territory, placing pressure on relationships at the very moment they need the most grace. These expectations are often not intentional; they form out of fear, exhaustion, or a deep desire for relief. But when they don't align with reality, they create fractures in connection.

Common stress-shaped expectations include:
• **Unrealistic Support Expectations**: Expecting a partner, friend, or colleague to carry the full weight of the stress—emotionally, mentally, or practically—while offering little in return. This can create burnout and imbalance in the relationship.
• **Expectation of Unwavering Stability**: Believing that the relationship should stay perfectly steady despite external pressures. This overlooks the fact that stress affects both people differently and that relationships naturally shift under strain.

• **Expectation of Instant Solutions**: Wanting immediate answers, quick fixes, or emotional relief without recognizing that many stressors—financial crises, health issues, workplace instability—require time, patience, and shared effort to work through.

When expectations become misaligned with reality, stress transforms into disappointment, frustration, and conflict. Small misunderstandings feel larger. Emotional distance grows. The relationship begins to feel unstable—not because love or commitment is weak, but because the weight of unrealistic expectations makes connection harder to sustain.

Healthy expectations during stressful seasons require honesty, partnership, and compassion. When both people understand what is realistic and what is not, stress becomes something they navigate together rather than something that pulls them apart.

External Stressors and Assumptions: *Misjudging the Impact of Stress*

External stress doesn't just weigh on our emotions—it distorts the assumptions we make about the people around us. When we're overwhelmed, it becomes easy to misinterpret silence, difference, or distance as neglect or indifference. Instead of seeking clarity, we fill in the gaps with assumptions that reflect our fears more than reality. These unspoken beliefs create emotional distance at the exact moment when connection is needed most.

Common stress-driven assumptions include:
• "They don't care because they're not reacting like I am." Assuming that someone's different coping style means they lack empathy or concern. In reality, people handle stress in deeply personal ways—some get quiet, others become task-oriented, and some shut down to avoid emotional overload.

• "I have to handle this alone."
Assuming that asking for help is a burden, a weakness, or an invitation for judgment. This assumption isolates people, preventing them from receiving support that is actually available.

• "If they loved me, they'd know what I need."
Assuming that support should be instinctive. This belief ignores the truth that needs must be communicated clearly, especially during stressful seasons when emotional signals become harder to read.

These assumptions shut down communication and widen the emotional gap. Instead of building understanding, they create confusion, resentment, and loneliness. The external stressor becomes heavier—not because the situation itself worsened, but because the story we told ourselves about another person's response added an extra layer of strain.

Breaking this pattern requires humility, clarity, and the willingness to ask rather than assume. When we communicate our needs and seek to understand others' responses, stress becomes something shared instead of something that divides.

Breaking the Cycle

Because external stressors affect our attitude, expectations, and assumptions, breaking the cycle requires deliberate and thoughtful adjustments in how we show up for one another. The first shift begins with attitude. When stress rises, it's easy to slip into blame, withdrawal, or emotional shutdown. But adopting a mindset rooted in teamwork, patience, and shared resilience reframes the challenge. Instead of seeing stress as something tearing the relationship apart, you begin approaching it as something you navigate side by side.

Equally important is reexamining your expectations. Stress impacts people differently—what overwhelms one person might barely rattle another. Healthy relationships require the flexibility to honor these differences. Support cannot be one-sided or rigid; it must evolve with the situation and with the people involved. When both individuals recognize that stress changes the emotional landscape, expectations naturally shift into something more realistic, compassionate, and sustainable.

Another essential step is confronting the assumptions that stress tends to magnify. Under pressure, the mind fills in blanks quickly and often inaccurately. Instead of assuming someone should "just know" what you need, or assuming their quietness signals indifference, communicate openly. Express what you are feeling, ask for clarity, and remember that love and care are shown in countless ways—not all of them match your own style or timing. Breaking the cycle means choosing dialogue over silence and understanding over assumption.

External stressors will always exist; they are an unavoidable part of life. But when we face them with intention—adjusting our attitude, refining our expectations, and questioning the assumptions that rise during difficult seasons—stress becomes something that strengthens connection instead of weakening it. Relationships become sturdier, more resilient, and better equipped to withstand whatever life brings next.

Reflection Activity

Life will always present us with things to worry about—***ALWAYS.*** And like most people, I've been guilty of allowing external stressors to seep into my life and relationships. My greatest stress has always been my children's safety. When they were young, I had control. But once they became adults and I could no longer keep my thumb on them, my stress didn't disappear—it only evolved.

That anxiety was all-consuming. It followed me into my work, into meetings where I struggled to stay present, into moments where I stepped out to take their calls, feeling as if everything in my life had to function around this one fear. It wasn't just stress—it was control masquerading as concern. And at one point, my relationship with my son became toxic because of it. I cried at the mere thought of him, overwhelmed by worry, all while I was living on the other side of the world in the Middle East.

Thankfully, I was surrounded by incredibly understanding and empathetic people—an absolute blessing. But what truly needed to change was my attitude and expectations.

We rarely stop to consider one undeniable truth: worry changes nothing. ***Not one thing.***

Tears of stress won't alter a situation. Anxiety won't fix a problem. And withdrawing from others because of stress will only leave you isolated and alone. Much of our stress comes from the unrealistic expectation that we should be able to control outcomes. But the reality is, life doesn't work that way. The Bible wisely reminds us:

"Who of you by worrying can add a single hour to his life?" – Luke 12:25

"Which of you by worrying can add one cubit to his height?" – Matthew 6:27

Beyond the toll it takes on us personally, stress does something else—it can become a silent burden on our loved ones, damaging our relationships. We think our stress is our own, but in reality, the weight of it spills over onto those closest to us. Our children, partners, friends, and colleagues feel it in ways we don't always recognize. Our preoccupation with problems can make us emotionally unavailable, impatient, or distant. And when we expect others to share in our worry, we unknowingly place a strain on them.

I had to make a choice—to shift my attitude, let go of the stressor that was breaking me down emotionally, and change my expectations of how things "should" be. Release control! And in time, everything worked itself out. Our relationship is now strong, but I had to let go first and allow him to live his life, at his pace, being accountable for himself.

Stressors come in many forms. For me, it was my children. At one time in life, I didn't want them in the same car together! What if something happened…to both of them? Unnecessary stress! I get it now!

For others, it's finances, overwhelming workloads, health concerns, or personal struggles. But what they all have in common is this: we allow them to control us because of our expectations and mindset. We convince ourselves that if we just think about it enough, we'll figure out a way to fix it. But the truth is, every moment spent stressing is a moment subtracted from your life.

Science confirms this—chronic stress takes a severe toll on both physical and mental health. It raises the risk of heart disease, weakens the immune system, impacts memory and decision-making, and fuels anxiety and depression. But beyond that, stress can erode the very relationships we hold most dear. If you've ever snapped at a loved one, withdrawn from friends, or felt resentment because others don't seem as worried as you, then your stress is not just affecting you—it's affecting them too.

That was me. Is it you?

A Plan of Action: The Only Way to Combat Stress
There is only one real way to combat stress—a plan of action. Without a plan, stress will continue to control you. But when you take proactive steps, you regain power over your mind, emotions, and life.

And it starts with changing your attitude and expectations. You must accept that you cannot control everything, but you can control your response to it.

Here's how to start:

- **Identify Your Stressor** – Be honest with yourself. What is the root cause of your stress? Name it.
- **Acknowledge What You Can and Cannot Control** – Some things are beyond your power. Let them go.
- **Change Your Attitude Toward It** – Instead of resisting the situation, ask yourself: How can I adjust my expectations and approach?
- **Ask for Help** – You don't have to carry your burdens alone. Seek support from your community.
- **Set Boundaries** – Protect your time, energy, and peace. Say no when necessary.
- **Practice Letting Go** – Say your peace, release it, and trust the process.
- **Consider How Your Stress Affects Others** – Are you unintentionally placing your burdens on those around you? How can you shift your energy to preserve your relationships?

What stressor can you let go of today? What plan of action can you put in place right now? Write it down. Make it real. Take the first step toward reclaiming your peace and protecting your relationships.

3K. Cultural or Value Differences:

Differences in values, beliefs, traditions, or life priorities can create significant friction in relationships of every kind. When people come from different cultural backgrounds or hold contrasting worldviews, misunderstandings can occur long before anyone realizes what went wrong. What one person views as respectful, another may interpret as rude. What one sees as commitment, another may see as control. Without understanding, curiosity, and a willingness to bridge the gap, these differences can slowly erode trust, connection, and collaboration.

In workplaces, cultural or value differences can disrupt productivity and teamwork. Misinterpreted communication styles, unspoken norms, or conflicting expectations about leadership and accountability often lead to unnecessary tension. In social spaces, the damage can be even greater. When we fail to invest the effort to understand another person's background or worldview, we miss the opportunity to grow, to expand our perspective, and to become more empathetic human beings.

Let's address the elephant in the room—right here on the page. Seeking to understand someone else's culture does **not** require you to abandon your own. It does not mean you must adopt their values, traditions, or ways of life. But too often, people react defensively to difference. We get our emotions tangled, our perspectives rigid, our "knickers in a knot," simply because someone else's way of being in the world does not look like ours. If we're honest, that reaction exposes something uncomfortable: a certain selfishness, a belief—however subconscious—that our way is the default, the standard, the norm.

When relationships end because of cultural or value differences, it is a profound loss. Not just for the individuals involved, but for the potential growth that was never allowed to happen. The more we listen, learn, and attempt to understand the experiences of others, the better human beings we become. The world is vast—different time zones, continents, rituals, customs, and belief systems stretching farther than we could travel in a lifetime. That diversity is not a threat; it is a gift. A beautiful, expansive, world-shaping gift.

And if diversity doesn't strike you as beautiful yet, I hope that as you continue reading, you will find your perspective widening. I hope your assumptions about "other people" begin to soften. Because when we let go of the fear of difference, we gain the ability to see people as they truly are—not as caricatures of our assumptions, but as complex, remarkable individuals deserving of understanding.

Cultural or value differences primarily align with **assumptions**, because they influence how we interpret behaviors, communication styles, and relational norms. But they also shape our **expectations**, determining what we believe others "should" do, and our **attitude**, revealing whether we approach differences with openness or resistance. When we shift these internal forces, cultural differences stop being barriers and become bridges—pathways to connection, wisdom, and mutual respect.

Cultural or Value Differences and Assumptions:

The Root of Misunderstandings

Cultural and value differences often plant unconscious assumptions about what is "normal," "respectful," or "right" in relationships. These assumptions become the invisible rules we expect others to follow—even when they've never been spoken out loud. When two people carry different internal rulebooks, misunderstandings become almost inevitable. What feels natural to one may feel confusing or even offensive to the other. And when these unspoken expectations collide, frustration, misinterpretation, and conflict begin to take root.

Consider some of the assumptions that commonly arise when cultural or value systems collide:

- **"If they don't express love the way I do, they don't care."**
  This assumes that affection must look the same everywhere—as if love languages, emotional expression, or gestures of care are universal. In reality, cultural traditions shape *how* people show love, not whether they feel it.
- **"They should prioritize family the way I do."**
  This assumes that family roles and obligations follow the same pattern across communities. Some cultures prioritize extended family involvement; others emphasize independence. Neither is right or wrong—they are simply different.
- **"Their approach to work-life balance is wrong."**
  This assumes that one view of ambition, rest, or responsibility is superior. Cultures hold vastly different beliefs about productivity, leisure, and success. What looks like laziness to one person may look like emotional health to another.
- **"Good communication means being direct (or indirect)."**
  This assumes that only one communication style is effective or respectful. Some cultures value straightforward expression; others emphasize tone, timing, and subtlety. Both approaches are valid—they simply reflect different histories and social norms.

When people operate from rigid cultural assumptions, they filter every action, comment, and decision through their own worldview. This creates a distorted understanding of the other person—one based on comparison rather than curiosity. Over time, these misunderstandings can harden into resentment. People begin withdrawing not because the relationship is toxic, but because the *interpretation* of each other's behavior has become skewed by assumptions.

Expanding beyond these assumptions requires humility, openness, and a willingness to acknowledge that our personal norms are not universal truths. When we learn to ask questions instead of making judgments, cultural and value differences stop feeling like threats. They become invitations—opportunities to understand another human being more deeply and to broaden our own sense of the world.

Cultural or Value Differences and Expectations:
What We Think Others Should Follow

Cultural backgrounds and personal value systems quietly shape the expectations we place on the people in our lives. These influences determine what we consider "normal," "respectful," or "appropriate"—often long before we realize we're holding those standards at all. Every culture, family, and community teaches its own interpretation of roles, responsibilities, communication, and emotional expression. When two people come together—whether in romance, friendship, work, or family—they bring those internalized scripts with them.

Trouble arises when these expectations stay unspoken. When we assume others will naturally follow the same rules we were raised with, we set the stage for misunderstanding. What feels obvious or intuitive to one person may feel foreign to another. And when those hidden expectations collide, tension and disappointment can surface—not because someone is wrong, but because they are different.

In **romantic relationships**, this often shows up as one partner expecting the other to behave according to traditional or modern gender roles. Someone raised in a household where one partner handled finances while the other managed the home may unconsciously expect that dynamic to repeat. Their partner, shaped by a different upbringing, may expect shared responsibilities or a more fluid division of labor. Without conversation, both partners can feel misunderstood, unappreciated, or even judged.

In **friendships**, cultural norms heavily influence what closeness should look like. Some cultures value deep emotional sharing, frequent communication, and open-door availability. Others honor independence, personal space, and minimal emotional demands. When friends operate from different norms, one may feel smothered while the other feels abandoned—not because either is wrong, but because their expectations were shaped in different worlds.

In **the workplace**, cultural values impact how people perceive leadership, communication, and professionalism. A manager from a direct-communication culture may interpret indirect feedback as evasive or unclear. An employee from a high-context culture may see bluntness as disrespectful or aggressive. Work ethic expectations differ as well—some prioritize speed, others precision; some value hierarchy, others collaboration. When these differences go unnamed, teams can struggle with misalignment and resentment, even when everyone is trying their best.

Within **family dynamics**, cultural expectations are often the strongest. Some families elevate duty, loyalty, and collective identity—where decisions must honor the family unit. Others prioritize independence, self-expression, and personal boundaries. These differences influence everything from caregiving roles to holiday traditions to how conflict is handled. When family members hold unspoken, conflicting values, misunderstandings can quickly escalate into long-standing emotional distance.

Ultimately, unrealistic or unspoken expectations—especially those rooted in culture or deeply held values—create fertile ground for frustration. They can blind us to the beauty of diverse perspectives and the possibility of learning from one another. When we slow down and recognize that people are shaped by different histories, we make room for curiosity instead of criticism, grace instead of judgment, and connection instead of conflict.

Cultural or Value Differences and Attitude: *How We Approach Differences*

How we *approach* cultural and value differences often determines whether those differences become bridges that strengthen relationships or barriers that quietly divide them. Our attitude acts as the filter through which we interpret unfamiliar behaviors, beliefs, and traditions. Two people can encounter the same cultural contrast—one feeling curious and open, the other feeling threatened or judgmental—and their relational outcomes will be drastically different. In this way, attitude is the deciding factor between growth and conflict.

An **open-minded attitude** invites connection. People who hold this posture see cultural differences as opportunities to stretch their understanding, learn from others, and expand their worldview. They approach unfamiliar customs or values with humility rather than defensiveness, seeking to understand before forming conclusions. This openness often leads to deeper appreciation, stronger communication, and more meaningful relationships.

A **rigid or judgmental attitude**, however, closes the door before dialogue even begins. When someone believes their cultural norms or personal values are the "correct" or superior standard, they may overlook the validity and richness of perspectives that differ from their own. This attitude can show up subtly—through dismissiveness, impatience, or quiet condescension—or overtly through criticism and intolerance. Over time, rigidity creates emotional distance and fuels division.

A **defensive attitude** emerges when cultural differences are interpreted as threats. Instead of seeing diversity as an exchange of ideas, the person feels personally challenged, as if any deviation from their norm undermines their identity or beliefs. This can lead to arguments, withdrawal, or a refusal to engage in meaningful conversation. Defense blocks curiosity, and without curiosity, understanding becomes impossible.

An **adaptable attitude**, on the other hand, reflects maturity and relational wisdom. People who adopt this posture learn how to honor their own values while also respecting the values of others. They do not abandon their convictions, but they recognize that coexistence requires flexibility, empathy, and a willingness to meet others halfway. Adaptability leads to smoother interactions, reduced conflict, and an environment where everyone feels seen and valued.

When cultural or value differences meet a rigid attitude, the result is often exclusion, conflict, or emotional disconnection. But when those same differences encounter openness, adaptability, and humility, relationships can transform into spaces where diversity becomes a source of enrichment rather than division.

Breaking the Cycle

Because cultural and value differences shape the assumptions we make, the expectations we hold, and the attitudes we bring into relationships, breaking the cycle of misunderstanding requires intentional self-awareness. Growth begins when we slow down long enough to examine the mental scripts we inherited—scripts that may no longer serve us or the relationships we want to build.

Breaking the cycle first requires challenging our assumptions. We must recognize that "different" is not synonymous with "wrong" or "disrespectful." Differences reflect diversity—layers of history, upbringing, belief, and identity that deserve exploration rather than judgment. When we interrupt the automatic stories we tell ourselves about others, we create space for truth to replace bias.

It also involves adjusting our expectations. People do not operate from the same cultural frameworks, emotional norms, or value systems. What feels natural or obvious to one person may feel unfamiliar or uncomfortable to another. Healthy expectations acknowledge this reality. They allow us to engage others with clarity, communication, and flexibility instead of demanding conformity to our personal standards.

Finally, breaking the cycle requires shifting our attitude. When we move from defensiveness to curiosity, from rigidity to respect, from superiority to humility, we create conditions where genuine connection can flourish. An adaptable attitude allows us to honor our own values while appreciating the values of others, strengthening our capacity for empathy and relational growth.

When we choose openness over assumption and understanding over judgment, cultural and value differences no longer divide us. Instead, they enrich our relationships, deepen our connections, and expand the way we see the world—and one another.

Reflection Activity

My husband is Danish—born and raised in Denmark—which is very different from my African American upbringing in the United States. Our roles and responsibilities differed, the way we celebrated holidays differed, and most impactfully, the way we communicated was different. Some areas were a challenge, but our relationship meant far more than those differences, so we faced them one by one. Both of us are world travelers who value diversity—but living it daily was an adjustment. We now embrace each other's traditions and celebrations, and we make a conscious effort to reflect on how we communicate, staying intentional about what matters most: our union.

Have you ever experienced an activity, celebration, or way of doing something—whether at work, in friendship, or in a romantic relationship—that was completely different from how you or your family would approach it? Did those differences ever make you hesitate or choose not to participate? Do the contrasts between you and a friend, spouse, or loved one sometimes create tension or misunderstanding? If so, consider this: perhaps those differences aren't obstacles, but opportunities—unique invitations to grow, learn, and turn what divides you into a deeper blessing.

3L. Financial Stress and Money Conflicts

Money is one of the most persistent and emotionally charged stressors in relationships—not only in romantic partnerships, but across families, friendships, business collaborations, and team dynamics. Financial strain has a way of magnifying every insecurity, every difference in worldview, and every unspoken expectation two people bring to the table. It's not just about dollars and cents; it's about what money symbolizes—security, freedom, control, comfort, love, or survival.

For some, financial stress looks like bills piling up faster than paychecks can cover them. For others, it's the constant pressure of rising expenses, unstable income, or unexpected emergencies that threaten to wipe out months of progress. Even when money *is* coming in, the way each person relates to that money can create friction. One might be a disciplined saver who finds comfort in watching their account grow, while the other is a spontaneous spender who believes life is meant to be enjoyed in real time.

These contrasting financial personalities often stem from deeper stories and experiences. One partner might operate from a belief that you "can't take it with you," so you might as well enjoy life now—travel, eat well, give generously, live fully, and trust that tomorrow will take care of itself. Another might feel a deep responsibility to prepare for the future—to save for retirement, ensure long-term stability, and build a financial cushion for the unexpected seasons of life when work slows down or stops altogether.

Both mindsets make sense within the context of someone's lived experience. But when these philosophies collide in the same relationship, the tension can feel overwhelming. What brings one person joy may trigger anxiety in the other. What feels responsible to one may feel restrictive or joyless to the other. And without honest communication, even well-intentioned decisions can be misinterpreted as careless, controlling, or inconsiderate.

Financial stress also has a way of transforming everyday conversations into emotional minefields. A simple question like, *"Did you really need to buy that?"* can trigger shame, defensiveness, or resentment. On the other side, silence or avoidance around money can be equally damaging—leading to hidden spending, unspoken fears, or escalating frustration. Before long, the budget isn't the only thing under strain; the relationship itself begins to feel fragile. Trust develops hairline cracks. Communication becomes cautious. And emotional intimacy takes a back seat to survival mode.

But here's the truth that often gets overlooked: money is not the relationship destroyer. Money is the *visible* stressor—the "smoke" rising to the surface. The real fire beneath that smoke is fueled by attitudes, assumptions, and expectations.

People carry powerful attitudes about money: whether it's a tool or a burden, a symbol of success or a reminder of scarcity. They bring assumptions: about who should manage it, how it should be spent, and what financial responsibility looks like. And they hold expectations—often unspoken—about how partners, family members, or colleagues should handle financial decisions.

Financial stress tends to align most strongly with expectations, but it is deeply shaped—often silently—by the attitudes and assumptions we've absorbed over a lifetime. When those internal patterns go unexamined, disagreements about money become symbolic battles about respect, responsibility, security, and identity.

Financial Stress, Money Conflicts, and Expectations: *The Unspoken Money Rules*

Most money conflicts have very little to do with the actual amount in the bank and far more to do with the unspoken rules people carry about how money should work. Every person grows up with an invisible "money script"—a set of attitudes, lessons, and beliefs absorbed from family, culture, and personal experience. These scripts quietly shape expectations long before a relationship even forms. Some people grow up believing that "real adults don't live paycheck to paycheck," while others learn that survival and resourcefulness matter more than financial perfection. One person may internalize the message, "If you loved me, you wouldn't stress me with bills," connecting financial stability to emotional security. Another inherits the belief that "the man should provide," linking identity and worth to earning power. Others adopt the stance, "If I earn it, I spend it how I want," seeing money as autonomy rather than shared responsibility.

These internal money rules rarely get spoken aloud, yet people enforce them as if everyone else received the same training. In romantic relationships, for example, one partner may assume that finances will automatically be merged and handled as a unified team, while the other assumes that financial independence will continue even after commitment. Without conversation, both believe their approach is the obvious or "correct" one, and when the other person doesn't comply, it feels like betrayal rather than a misunderstanding.

In family relationships, expectations around money can become even more complex. Adult children may expect financial rescue during hardships, assuming parents will always step in as they once did. Meanwhile, parents may expect gratitude, responsibility, or repayment—believing that support should be met with appreciation and maturity. These mismatched expectations can turn acts of generosity into breeding grounds for resentment when either side feels taken for granted or unfairly judged.

Even in the workplace, unspoken money rules show up in subtle but powerful ways. Leaders may expect employees to separate personal financial struggles from professional performance, operating under the belief that work should remain unaffected by life's pressures. Employees, however, may expect empathy, flexibility, or understanding when faced with rising costs, family emergencies, or economic instability. When neither side communicates their expectations, frustration grows—leaders feel blindsided, and employees feel misunderstood.

When expectations about money are never named, they eventually become weaponized. The disappointment often begins with a silent accusation: *"You should know better."* But because the "rules" were never actually discussed, both sides feel wronged and neither feels heard. Over time, these unmet expectations harden into resentment, turning financial stress into emotional distance and relational strain.

Financial Stress, Money Conflicts and **Attitude**: *What Money "Means" to Us*

Money is never just money. Even though it appears to be a simple exchange of dollars and decisions, it is often wrapped tightly around identity, security, and self-worth. Our attitude toward finances shapes how we interpret every money conversation, every purchase, and every moment of financial pressure. For some, money represents safety—a buffer against uncertainty, a reassurance that no matter what happens, they will be okay. For others, money symbolizes freedom—the ability to make choices, take risks, and live without feeling trapped. Still, others see money as a marker of status or success, something that validates their hard work or signals that they are "doing well" in life.

When financial stress appears, these meanings come rushing to the surface. A disagreement about spending or saving is no longer just about the budget; it strikes at the core of what each person believes money represents. If money equals safety, any unexpected bill or impulse purchase can feel like danger. If money equals freedom, strict budgeting can feel suffocating. If money equals status, financial struggles may trigger shame or fear of judgment. Suddenly, the conflict is not about numbers—it's about identity.

These internal attitudes heavily influence how people respond during financial tension. Blame may show up, with one partner accusing the other: *"We're broke because of you."* Superiority can follow, where the person who believes they are better with money assumes they should automatically take control. And for many, shame looms quietly in the background. Someone may fear that revealing their true income, debt, or financial mistakes will change how others see them. This fear creates secrecy, avoidance, and emotional walls.

Once shame and blame enter the conversation, financial planning stops being a joint effort and becomes a battlefield. Instead of working together, partners, family members, or colleagues begin protecting themselves—guarding their choices, withholding information, and defending their financial identity. The real conflict becomes not "How do we manage our money?" but "Do you respect me? Do you trust me? Do you see my worth even when my finances are imperfect?"

When attitudes about money remain unexamined, financial stress becomes personal—deeply personal. But when people understand the emotional meanings behind their financial reactions, they gain the power to move from conflict to collaboration.

Financial Stress, Money Conflicts and Assumptions: *The Stories We Make Up*

Money is one of the easiest and most common places for assumptions to grow unchecked. Because finances are so deeply tied to fear, pride, and personal history, people often fill in the blanks with their own interpretations rather than seeking clarity. When someone spends differently than we do, we may assume it reflects their priorities—or their lack of concern for ours. When someone avoids talking about money, we may assume they are hiding something, or that their silence means agreement. These assumptions feel real, even logical, because they are shaped by our own experiences, anxieties, and expectations.

But financial assumptions are rarely accurate. One person may think, *"If they cared, they wouldn't spend like that,"* translating a purchase into a lack of love or responsibility. Another person might silently carry debt and assume, *"If I tell the truth, they'll leave,"* believing honesty will cost them connection. Someone might look at a friend or partner with a stable income and assume they are fine financially, never realizing the private pressures, obligations, or financial wounds that aren't visible on the surface. And perhaps most damaging, people often assume that silence equals consent—that if the other person has not objected, criticized, or questioned a financial decision, they must be perfectly aligned with it.

These unspoken stories create distance long before any real discussion happens. Instead of talking through fears, desires, or financial realities, people rely on assumptions to interpret behavior. They project their own meaning onto someone else's choices. Without realizing it, they turn internal narratives into "truths" that guide how they interact. This prevents the honest money conversations that could bring understanding and partnership.

When assumptions dominate, financial conflict becomes inevitable—not because the numbers don't add up, but because the relationship becomes filled with unspoken fears, hidden worries, and misinterpreted intentions. Clear communication could solve much of this tension, but as long as assumptions take the place of questions, the cycle of misunderstanding continues.

Breaking the Cycle

If finances are the smoke, then our attitudes, assumptions, and expectations about money are the fire burning beneath it. The real conflict rarely comes from the numbers themselves; it comes from the meanings, fears, and unspoken rules we attach to those numbers. To break the cycle, we must be willing to confront the internal patterns that fuel financial tension long before the bills arrive or the budget conversation begins.

Breaking the pattern starts with clarifying expectations. Instead of silently enforcing your own rules about spending, saving, giving, or debt, bring those expectations into the light. Honest conversations about financial values—what matters, what feels stressful, what feels safe—can prevent misunderstandings that snowball into resentment. When partners, families, or teams create a shared plan instead of operating from individual, unspoken standards, unity replaces conflict.

The next step is **checking your attitude**. This requires courage and humility. Ask yourself whether you are using money to control, punish, or prove something—intentionally or not. Are financial decisions becoming weapons in arguments? Is your tone revealing fear, frustration, or superiority? When money becomes a tool for power instead of partnership, no budget system will restore peace. But when we view money as a shared resource—something that supports stability, vision, and collective wellbeing—the entire emotional tone of the conversation shifts.

Finally, we must **challenge our assumptions**. Instead of filling in the blanks with the worst possible story, we learn to ask better questions. A simple, "Can you help me understand your thinking behind this?" opens a door that "What were you thinking?" instantly slams shut. Assumptions thrive in silence, but they lose power in honest dialogue. Curiosity heals what judgment destroys.

Money does not have to be a constant source of tension or emotional exhaustion. When we bring honesty, humility, and shared goals to the table, finances become a place of partnership rather than pain. The numbers may change, circumstances may fluctuate, but a relationship built on clarity and compassion can withstand financial stress—and even grow stronger because of it.

Reflection Activity

Let's get real—money is personal. And if you've ever felt your stomach twist while opening a bill or checking your balance, you are far from alone. I've lived through seasons where I was juggling more bills than blessings, times when I had the degrees, the title, the responsibilities—but behind the scenes, I was still doing financial gymnastics just to keep everything afloat. There were moments when stress about money leaked into my tone, my patience, and my relationships. Not because I didn't care about the people around me, but because I was scared. Fear will always try to speak louder than faith, especially when it comes to money.

Take a moment and reflect:

When you think about money, what emotion shows up first—fear, shame, control, gratitude, or something else? What unspoken expectations do you hold about how money *should* be handled in your relationships? Have finances ever caused you to pull away, shut down, or lash out at someone you love? Is your conflict really about the numbers—or about what those numbers seem to mean about you or them?

Activity:
Write down one money-related tension (past or present) that has impacted a relationship. This can be at work, or at home. Then ask yourself:
Was the real issue attitude, assumption, or expectation?

Circle one. Then write one step you can take to bring more honesty and teamwork into that area—whether it's a conversation, a budget, or simply an apology.

3M. Loss of Connection and Drifting Apart

Not every relationship ends with fireworks or a dramatic explosion. Some end quietly—through the slow, silent drift that happens when life gets busy, hearts get tired, or emotional distance goes unaddressed. You stop talking the way you used to. The inside jokes fade. The texts grow shorter. You begin showing up in the same house, office, or Zoom room, yet emotionally you feel worlds apart. The loss of connection starts subtly, almost imperceptibly, but over time it becomes just as destructive as a major betrayal.

The tragedy is that many relationships don't shatter in a single moment—they erode. And erosion is deceptive. It is slow, quiet, and almost invisible until one day you look up and realize the entire landscape of the relationship has changed. You wonder, *What happened? Didn't we see the small signs?* Most of the time, those signs were there—we were simply too overwhelmed, distracted, emotionally flooded, or neurologically dysregulated to notice. When our nervous systems are operating in survival mode, our capacity for presence, curiosity, and emotional attunement narrows, and connection becomes one of the first casualties.

I have been intentional in this book not to be overly expressive about my relationship with Christ, because I wanted the focus to remain on universal relationship truths. But here, I must say this plainly: relationships are covenants, especially marriage. And even in the workplace, we sometimes treat a contract or employment agreement with a covenant-like seriousness. Yes, there are conditions that may void or end that covenant. Yes, there are times when separation is necessary, healthy, or unavoidable. But more often than not, a covenant calls us to do what it takes to sustain the relationship—to honor the commitment, to finish what we started, to fulfill the responsibilities we agreed upon.

If you are bored, address it. If you are tired, find rest and make space. If you feel empty—no longer fueled by the same purpose that once held you together—expand your purpose. Rekindle your connection. Rediscover your partnership. Reignite your commitment to show up with intention.

Here's the truth: it is not the loss of connection itself that destroys relationships. Disconnection is the smoke, not the fire. Underneath that smoke is a slow-burning combination of attitude, assumptions, and expectations—the very patterns that suffocate intimacy long before we notice the distance. And beneath those patterns, as we explored in Chapter 2, is the nervous system's ongoing search for safety, certainty, and belonging. When that system is overwhelmed or threatened, emotional withdrawal often becomes an unconscious form of self-protection.

The drifting didn't happen overnight. The silence didn't suddenly appear. The numbness didn't arrive out of nowhere.

It accumulated. It compounded. It grew in the shadows of unspoken needs, misinterpreted motives, emotional fatigue, and nervous system overload. And by the time the distance becomes visible, the root causes have already been at work for months or even years.

But naming it—seeing it clearly—is the first step toward rebuilding. Because once you recognize that drifting apart is the symptom, not the disease, you gain the power to heal the relationship at its source.

Loss of Connection and Drifting Apart & Attitude: *When We Stop Showing Up*

Connection never sustains itself automatically. It isn't a self-running machine; it is a living, breathing part of a relationship that requires presence, intention, and engagement. The moment we start assuming the relationship will "run on its own," we begin to drift. Our attitude—how we show up, how we prioritize the other person, how we view the relationship—determines whether we continue nurturing the bond or quietly pull away without realizing it. Disconnection rarely begins with a dramatic moment. It starts with a subtle shift in our posture: the slow erosion of effort, curiosity, emotional regulation, and care.

When stress, burnout, or emotional exhaustion tax our nervous system, showing up fully becomes neurologically harder. We may not consciously choose disengagement, but our body defaults to energy conservation, withdrawal, or emotional numbing as a form of protection. Over time, that protective posture becomes relational distance.

Unhelpful attitudes often slip in unnoticed. Complacency whispers, *"We're fine. We've known each other forever. We don't need to talk about everything."* It convinces us that familiarity is a substitute for communication, that history can carry a relationship indefinitely. But even long-standing relationships cannot thrive on autopilot. Resignation is another silent threat. It sounds like, *"This is just how it is now. We've grown apart."* Instead of addressing the discomfort, we settle into emotional distance as if it were inevitable, convincing ourselves that nothing can be done. And then there's scorekeeping, the internal stance of, *"I'm not reaching out—they should call me first."* This attitude turns connection into a competition, where pride takes precedence over closeness and both people wait for the other to make the first move.

These attitudes gradually shift us from active participants in the relationship to passive observers. We stop pursuing. We stop checking in. We stop listening with intention. The relationship begins to mirror our withdrawal—conversations become shallow, affection becomes inconsistent, and emotional presence fades. What once felt like a partnership becomes parallel lives running beside each other with no true intersection.

Healthy relationships require a completely different posture—one that says, *"I value this connection enough to keep showing up—on purpose."* This mindset recognizes that love, friendship, teamwork, and commitment all demand nourishment. It understands that connection grows where effort is planted. When we approach relationships with an attitude of intentional presence, we breathe life back into the bond, replacing drift with engagement and restoring the closeness that once felt effortless.

Loss of Connection and Drifting Apart & Assumptions: *The Silent Stories We Tell*

When distance begins to creep into a relationship, we rarely sit in a place of calm neutrality. Instead, we fill the silence with stories—narratives shaped by our fears, insecurities, and past experiences. And as we explored in Chapter 2, when our nervous system senses uncertainty or threat, it seeks meaning quickly, often through assumptions that restore a sense of certainty—even if those stories are painful or inaccurate.

The human mind is quick to interpret gaps in communication as intentional, and when someone pulls back or becomes less available, our assumptions rush in to explain why. We tell ourselves, *"If they wanted me in their life, they'd make time,"* or, *"They're different now; they've changed."* We may quietly conclude, *"They don't need me anymore,"* or in workplace settings, *"My team must not care what I think—they never ask."* These assumptions feel real because they offer a sense of certainty in moments where we feel uncertain or vulnerable.

Sometimes these stories hold a measure of truth—but often, they don't. Life has seasons that reshape how much emotional, physical, and mental energy a person can offer. New jobs, demanding workloads, raising children, health challenges, caregiving responsibilities, burnout, and grief all affect availability and capacity. Someone may be overwhelmed, not uncaring. They may be stretched thin, not indifferent. They may be fighting a silent battle, not pulling away from the relationship intentionally. But assumptions rarely leave room for nuance. Instead, they reduce complex life circumstances into simplified stories that usually cast us as unwanted or unimportant.

This is where the danger lies. Overthinking can turn a temporary busy season into a long-term narrative of rejection. What began as a normal ebb in communication becomes interpreted as abandonment. A missed call becomes a sign of fading interest. A late reply becomes proof that the relationship no longer matters. Before long, the distance we're afraid of becomes a self-fulfilling prophecy—not because someone walked away, but because assumptions built emotional walls where there should have been curiosity and compassion.

Assumptions transform ordinary relational drift into emotional abandonment, even when no one has actually stepped out of the relationship. They distort reality, fuel insecurity, and magnify every gap in connection. And unless we challenge these silent stories, we risk losing relationships not because they ended—but because we convinced ourselves they already had.

Loss of Connection and Drifting Apart & Expectations: *When "How It Used to Be" Becomes the Enemy*

Loss of connection often cuts the deepest when we cling to an old version of the relationship—an earlier chapter we believe should still be happening, unchanged, untouched by time. Expectations become the silent rulers of our emotional world, shaping how we interpret every shift in closeness. We expect a friendship to feel the way it did in college, before careers, kids, and cross-country moves stretched everyone in different directions. We expect marriage to always carry the spark of the honeymoon phase, forgetting that love matures, deepens, and evolves through seasons that require far more than butterflies. We expect our team at work to maintain the same level of energy, connection, and camaraderie year after year, as if life circumstances, staffing changes, burnout, and personal demands never enter the picture.

When reality doesn't align with those idealized expectations, disappointment settles in quickly. Instead of appreciating the relationship as it is now—its new strengths, its new rhythms, its new opportunities—we become preoccupied with what feels lost. We focus on the gap between "how it used to be" and "how it is now," and that gap becomes a source of frustration, grief, or resentment. We start believing something must be wrong, when in truth, something may simply be *different*.

Unspoken expectations add even more pressure. We quietly tell ourselves, *"If we were really close, we'd talk every day,"* or, *"If they valued this team, they'd show up to every event."* In romantic relationships, we may think, *"If they loved me the way they used to, they'd still act like they did in the beginning."* These hidden standards turn natural relational evolution into perceived rejection. Instead of recognizing that people's capacities shift with life's demands, we interpret any change as fading interest or diminishing love.

This misunderstanding is one of the silent killers of connection. People grow, schedules change, responsibilities increase, and relationships must adapt. But when we insist that a relationship remain frozen in its earlier form, we set ourselves up for disappointment. We mistake evolution for decline. We confuse maturity with distance. We interpret normal shifts as personal wounds.

Sometimes we're not actually losing connection—we're resisting the relationship's opportunity to evolve. When we release the grip of outdated expectations, we create space for relationships to grow in healthier, more sustainable ways. We discover that connection doesn't have to look like it did before to be meaningful now. And in that acceptance, new intimacy, new rhythms, and new forms of closeness can emerge.

Breaking the Cycle

Because loss of connection is shaped by our attitudes, assumptions, and expectations, healing it requires an intentional recalibration of how we show up in the relationship. Distance doesn't close on its own; someone has to make the first shift. And that shift begins on the inside, long before any external changes happen—at the level of awareness, emotional regulation, and nervous system safety.

Healing starts with shifting your attitude. Instead of sliding into passivity—waiting for the other person to reach out, waiting for the closeness to magically return—you choose to move from passive to purposeful. You decide to be an active builder of connection rather than a quiet critic of what's missing. This mindset breathes life back into relationships that have been running on autopilot. It says, "I'm showing up with intention, even if the effort feels awkward or overdue."

The next step is to challenge your assumptions. When someone grows distant, it's easy to fill the silence with painful stories: *They don't care. They've changed. I'm not important anymore.* But those narratives often reveal more about our fears than the truth about the other person. Instead of defaulting to rejection, ask yourself, *"What else might be true about their season right now?"* They may be exhausted, overwhelmed, grieving, growing, or navigating pressures you know nothing about. Curiosity keeps the door open where assumptions try to slam it shut.

Finally, healing requires updating your expectations. Relationships evolve, and closeness evolves with them. What connection looked like in one season may not be sustainable in the next—and that doesn't mean the relationship is dying. It simply means it's changing. When we allow relationships to grow, stretch, and shift without demanding they resemble an old chapter, we create room for new, meaningful forms of connection. Different does not mean destroyed.

Sometimes reconnection happens through one vulnerable conversation—one moment of honesty that breaks months of silence. Other times, healing means grieving what once was and choosing to invest your energy into connections that are healthier, mutual, and life-giving. Both paths are valid. Both are healing. And both honor the truth that relationships thrive not by accident, but by intention.

Reflection Activity

Let's talk about drifting.

As a leader, mother, wife, friend, and educator, I've lived through seasons where my calendar was full—but my heart felt lonely. I've had stretches where I poured so much into work, ministry, and family that I suddenly looked up and realized, *"I'm surrounded by people... but I don't feel deeply connected to many of them right now."*

There were friendships that changed. People I used to talk to every day slowly became "once in a while" check-ins. Team members I loved working with moved on. My own life shifted—from single mom, to principal, to expat in the Middle East, to wife of a Danish husband, to "Dr. Moni Kay" traveling and teaching. Each new chapter brought blessings… and also a quiet, unspoken grief.

When we don't name that grief, we start telling ourselves dangerous stories: *Maybe I wasn't that important to them. Maybe I'm just meant to do life alone. Maybe deep connection just doesn't last.* None of those thoughts are from God. They come from fear, fatigue, and unprocessed loss.

Take a moment to reflect on your own life. Is there a relationship where you've felt a quiet drift—not because of betrayal, but because of busyness, transition, or unspoken tension? Notice the attitude you've adopted toward that relationship. Have you slipped into complacency, resentment, or resignation? Think about the assumptions you've made about why the other person pulled back. Have you decided they don't care, that you no longer matter, or that the relationship has run its course—without ever having an honest conversation? And consider the expectations you're still holding. Are you expecting the relationship to look like a previous season, even though both of you have changed?

Activity:
Choose one relationship—personal or professional—where you've felt connection slipping. On paper or in a journal, write out the story you've been telling yourself about why the distance exists. Then identify which of the three silent destroyers is most active there: **attitude**, **assumption**, or **expectation**. Finally, choose one small step you can take. That step might be a simple text, a coffee invite, or an honest conversation that says, "I miss you." Or, it might be a different kind of step: choosing to release the relationship with gratitude instead of bitterness, acknowledging what it was in its season without resenting what it no longer is.

Remember: loss of connection is not always a sign of failure. Sometimes it's a sign that a new chapter is beginning—one that invites you to be more intentional, more honest, and more aware of the attitudes, assumptions, and expectations shaping your relationships.

Conclusion: *Seeing the Truth Beneath the Stressors*

If you've made it through all of these relationship stressors—financial pressure, loss of connection, cultural/value clashes, conflict cycles, and everything in between—pause for a moment and acknowledge the strength it took to keep reading. These topics aren't light.

They hold real weight because they touch the core of who we are and how we love, lead, and relate to others. The fact that you stayed with this chapter says something powerful about you: you care enough about your relationships to understand them, examine them, and ultimately strengthen them. That matters.

What you've just explored is not theory pulled from thin air. These insights are grounded in decades of research across relationship psychology, marriage and family studies, attachment science, neuroscience, and organizational behavior. Esteemed experts like Dr. John Gottman, whose work revealed the warning signs and emotional patterns that predict relational breakdown; Dr. Sue Johnson, who illuminated how attachment needs shape adult love; and many others have consistently found the same truth echoed in their research: The stressor itself is rarely the reason relationships fall apart. It's how we interpret it, react to it, and internalize it.

Again and again, studies show that attitude, assumptions, and expectations are the hidden forces shaping how we respond under stress. In every case of relational rupture—from marriages and friendships to workplace teams—one of these three root causes sits at the center, while the other two quietly reinforce it. The argument wasn't the end of the relationship. The financial struggle wasn't the end. The silence wasn't the end. The cultural clash wasn't the end. These were *symptoms*—the smoke rising from a deeper fire.

Many readers believe the stressor itself is what breaks the relationship. It's understandable—we tend to focus on what we can see. But the research is clear:

Stressors don't destroy relationships.
Our responses do.

And our responses are shaped by the internal patterns we carry: the attitudes we adopt, the assumptions we make, and the expectations we enforce.

Now that you've walked through the major relationship stressors and uncovered the hidden forces beneath them, you're ready to take the next step. In the following section, we'll dive deeper into these three silent but powerful relationship destroyers. You'll see what the research says about **attitude**, **assumptions**, and **expectations**—how they form, how they influence every interaction, and how they can be transformed into tools for connection instead of sources of conflict.

Ahead, you'll also find a chart summarizing each stressor, its underlying root cause, and the resources and scholars whose work has been foundational in shaping this understanding. This will give you a clearer framework as we transition into the next part of the journey.

Take a breath. You made it through the hard part. Now, let's look at the truth beneath the stressors—and discover why changing the inside is what transforms the outside.

Evidence-Based:

Relationship Destroyer	Root Cause	Research
Lack of Communication	Assumptions	*The Journal of Social and Personal Relationships* (2012)
Dishonesty or Deception	Attitude	*Psychological Science* (2013) and *The Journal of Marriage and Family* (2011)
Unresolved Conflict	Attitude	According to research by Dr. John Gottman and *The Journal of Family Psychology* (2015)
Selfishness / Self-Centeredness	Attitude	*Personal Relationships* (2016) and *The Journal of Marriage and Family* (2013)
Jealousy and Insecurity	Assumptions	*Personal Relationships* (2001) and *The Journal of Social and Personal Relationships* (2015)
Lack of Empathy	Attitude	The *Journal of Marriage and Family* (2003)
Toxic Behavior and Abuse	Attitude	*Journal of Interpersonal Violence* (2009)
Lack of Boundaries	Expectations	*The Journal of Marriage and Family* (2010) and *Psychology of Relationships* (2014)
Trauma and Past Experiences	Assumptions	The *Journal of Family Psychology* (2010) *The American Journal of Family Therapy* (2015)
External Stressors	Attitude	Studies in *Psychology of Relationships* (2012) and *The Journal of Family Psychology* (2016)
Cultural or Value Differences	Assumptions	A study in *The Journal of Marriage and Family* (2015)
Financial Stress and Money Conflicts	Expectations	A financial issue, a relationship issue, or both? Journal of Financial Therapy,
Loss of Connection and Drifting Apart	Assumptions	*The disconnected couple.* Current Opinion in Psychology, 43,

Where do we go next.

Now that we've identified the major relationship stressors and traced them back to their true roots—attitude, assumptions, and expectations—we are ready to go deeper. The next three chapters turn our attention inward, because real relational transformation does not begin with fixing others or managing circumstances; it begins with the internal work we often overlook.

We start with **attitude** because it shapes everything—every interpretation we make, every reaction we have, and every emotional habit we carry into our relationships. Attitude determines how we experience the world long before logic or communication enters the conversation. It influences how we perceive safety, respond to threat, regulate emotion, and interpret the intentions of others. In this way, attitude is not simply a personality trait—it is a powerful psychological lens, deeply intertwined with our nervous system, emotional memory, and lived experiences.

Attitude is not assigned at birth, nor is it permanently fixed. It is fluid and evolving, shaped by genetics, upbringing, culture, trauma, belief systems, and the repeated choices we make every day. And the beautiful truth is this: the moment we recognize our ability to influence and shift our own attitude, we reclaim the power to change our relational outcomes. When we change the lens, we change the experience.

Chapter 2 revealed how attitude operates beneath the surface, driving our emotional responses long before we consciously recognize them. We explored how neuroception, trauma memory, emotional hijacking, and survival-based reactions shape our relational posture—especially under stress. Whether attitude is the root cause or a reinforcing factor, it colors how we respond to conflict, disappointment, vulnerability, pressure, and emotional risk.

We saw how it affects marriages, friendships, family systems, workplace culture, leadership dynamics, and even our relationship with ourselves.

Now, in **Chapter 4**, we move into the work of awareness and transformation. This chapter invites you to examine the posture of your heart, the patterns of your mind, and the emotional habits that shape how you connect with others. Through reflection, neuroscience-informed insight, and intentional growth practices, we will explore how self-awareness becomes the gateway to relational healing.

This is not about perfection. It is about alignment.

It is about learning to recognize what drives your reactions, what shapes your interpretations, and what patterns you unconsciously carry forward. Because when awareness increases, choice expands. And when choice expands, transformation becomes possible.

This chapter is your invitation to pause, reflect, and recalibrate—so the relationships you build moving forward are not shaped by unconscious patterns, but by intentional purpose, emotional wisdom, and relational clarity.

Chapter 4: The Power of Self-Awareness and Intentional Growth in *Shaping Attitudes & Impacting Relationships*

We begin with attitude because it colors every interpretation, every reaction, and every habit we bring into our relationships. Attitude is not assigned to us at birth, nor is it a fixed trait we are stuck with forever. It is dynamic—constantly shaped by our genetics, environment, experiences, stressors, reflections, **and the way our nervous system learns to respond to safety, threat, and connection**. When we recognize that we have the ability to influence and change our own attitude, we reclaim the power to build healthier relationships in every part of our lives. In fact, attitude is the most reliable predictor of success in anything we do.

In Chapter 2, we examined how attitude contributes to relationship breakdowns—often operating beneath conscious awareness. Whether it serves as the root cause or quietly intensifies the other destroyers, attitude always plays a role. It affects the way we communicate, the assumptions we make, the expectations we enforce, and the emotional posture we carry into every interaction. As neuroscience and trauma psychology reveal, our brains are constantly scanning for safety, threat, and belonging, shaping our reactions before logic ever enters the conversation. This is why attitude becomes so powerful: it is deeply connected to emotional regulation, past experience, and nervous system responses. From marriages and friendships to leadership and workplace culture, attitude determines not just how we react—but how others experience us.

In this chapter, we will look more closely at how self-awareness and intentional growth reshape our attitudes. This deeper work is not just about improving our relationships with others—it is about improving the relationship we have with ourselves.

The Role of Self-Awareness in Attitude Transformation

Self-awareness is the foundation of any lasting attitude transformation. It begins with recognizing our emotional responses, thought patterns, bodily sensations, and behavioral habits. The more attuned we become to ourselves, the more clearly we can understand how our attitudes have been shaped—by life experience, emotional memory, trauma, and stress—and how they affect those around us.

Here's the truth: we have "attitudes" toward nearly everything. The day of the week, the task in front of us, the tone someone uses, our level of exhaustion—any of these can influence our emotional state. Neuroscience confirms that our nervous system is constantly interpreting these cues, often outside conscious awareness. Becoming aware of these shifts is the first step in preventing negative attitudes from spilling into our relationships and daily interactions. And as uncomfortable as self-awareness can be, it is also liberating. It opens the door to becoming a healthier, more grounded version of ourselves.

Self-awareness empowers us to identify negative thought patterns, understand the deeper emotional roots of our attitudes, and recognize internal triggers before they take over. These insights help us respond rather than react, regulate emotion rather than escalate it, and approach challenges with clarity instead of frustration. Journaling, meditation, prayer, intentional solitude, breathwork, and mindful pausing all strengthen this awareness and create space for meaningful change.

Being Vulnerable

My attitude gets the best of me when I don't take time to care for myself. As a natural nurturer, I'm always doing something to make someone else's life easier or better—and honestly, I love that about myself. It's a gift God placed in me. But the downside is that I rarely pause long enough to care for me.

From the moment my eyes open, I'm on go-mode. I lead people all day, and because my leadership style centers on making life easier for others, I am constantly giving out energy. By the time I walk through the door at home, I immediately shift into family mode—laundry, dinner, errands, watering plants, responding to messages, planning the next day. Even during my drive home, my mind is racing through grocery lists and tasks I don't want to forget.

I adore my grandbabies and my grown children, and I show up for everything I can—sports, NJROTC events, Back-to-School nights, you name it—because I love them deeply. I think about my husband's meals, his health, and how to make his 4:30am mornings easier. I'm always busy, and truthfully, I enjoy it.

But when I don't build in time for my own soul, a heaviness settles in. My nervous system becomes overloaded. My emotional capacity shrinks. My attitude starts shifting. Those other relationship destroyers—assumptions and expectations—begin creeping in. I start assuming that no one sees what I do, or how I show up for everyone. I expect my husband to magically "know" what I need without telling him. And suddenly, I'm irritated, overwhelmed, and emotionally thin.

Hey there! Don't judge me—I recognize it now. That's growth.

What brings me back into alignment? Alone time. A museum visit. A slow walk through beach boutiques. A seasonal festival. My favorite Christian music with no one else around. These moments regulate my nervous system. They help my body exhale. They restore emotional balance and reconnect me to peace. I've learned that I must be intentional about protecting my mental and emotional space—especially because attitude determines the success or failure of nearly everything I touch.

The Power of Intentional Growth

Awareness is only the first step. Intentional growth is where change becomes real. Recognizing a negative attitude does not transform it; choosing to do something about it does.

I'll be honest: sometimes I stay in a funk longer than I'd like before realizing I need to recharge. But I've become quicker at identifying the signs—tight shoulders, racing thoughts, emotional irritability, mental fatigue. These are signals from my body and nervous system that something needs attention. Intentional growth requires a willingness to confront our patterns, replace unhelpful habits, and commit to consistent personal development.

Intentional growth includes setting clear intentions for change, building new habits that support emotional regulation, seeking support from trusted people or professionals when necessary, and committing to lifelong learning. It also means allowing our loved ones into the journey so they can hold space for us, lovingly point out our blind spots, and support our transformation.

Growth doesn't happen by accident—it happens because we choose it.

Implementing Self-Awareness and Growth in Relationships

Once we've recognized the need to adjust our attitudes, the next step is applying that awareness and growth to how we show up in our relationships. Whether the setting is intimate, social, or professional, our attitude communicates long before our words ever do. It shapes tone, presence, patience, emotional safety, and trust. When we learn to manage our attitudes with intention, the health of every relationship in our life begins to shift.

In Intimate Relationships

In marriage or committed partnerships, self-awareness starts with noticing our emotional reactions. Are we responding to our partner out of present reality, or out of past hurt, exhaustion, or frustration? It's important to pause and discern the difference. When we understand the "why" behind our attitude—whether it's disappointment, stress, fear, or something else—we can communicate more clearly and avoid projecting old wounds onto our partner.

Healthy partnerships also thrive on shared goals. When we talk about attitude, we're talking about the lens through which we interpret situations. Creating mutual goals around communication, empathy, responsibility, or patience helps both partners grow together instead of drifting apart. And where past issues linger, forgiveness becomes essential. Unresolved hurt feeds negative attitudes faster than anything else. Extending grace—to yourself and to your partner—creates space for healing and resets the emotional climate.

In Work Life

Workplaces reveal our attitudes in profound ways. A challenging project, a demanding supervisor, or a misunderstanding with a coworker can all trigger negative reactions. But self-awareness allows us to pause and reframe the moment. Instead of seeing obstacles as problems, we can choose to view them as opportunities for growth, leadership, or creativity.

Feedback is another powerful space for attitude transformation. When we receive input with openness instead of guarded defensiveness, we signal maturity, professionalism, and emotional intelligence. This posture strengthens credibility and builds trust among colleagues. And when challenges arise, shifting from blame to solution-focused thinking helps reduce tension and encourages collaboration. Attitude often sets the tone for an entire team, and cultivating a constructive mindset at work enhances both performance and relationships.

In Friendships

Friendships thrive on emotional safety, honesty, and mutual encouragement. Strong friendships aren't defined by how often you talk but by the quality of connection when you do. Open communication makes this possible—speaking truthfully about needs, concerns, or changes while also listening with empathy

Supporting growth in your friends is another way to cultivate healthy attitudes within relationships. We grow stronger together when we hold each other accountable, pray together, share wisdom, and cheer for one another's progress. I'm reminded of: where Jesus says:

You are the salt of the earth.
— *Matthew 5:13 (NIV)*

This reminds us to influence others with grace, kindness, and steadiness. Gratitude also reinforces healthy attitudes—when we intentionally appreciate the beauty in our friendships, our hearts soften and connection deepens.

Conclusion: The Ongoing Journey of Attitude Growth

Transforming our attitude is not a single accomplishment—it is a lifelong journey. We cannot rewrite our genetics or erase our past, but we can take responsibility for how we think, how we process, and how we respond. Through self-awareness and intentional growth, we gain the ability to shift our internal landscape and cultivate healthier, more peaceful relationships.

One of the most valuable skills in this journey is learning to **pause**. When something triggers us, the instinct is to react immediately—but once a word is spoken or an action taken, it cannot be taken back. The pause allows space for awareness, clarity, and intentionality. It helps us identify which stressor was activated and choose a response that aligns with our peace instead of our pressure.

Our attitudes shape how we interact with the world. They influence how we perceive others, how we handle conflict, and how we navigate challenges. The more we invest in cultivating positive, grounded attitudes, the more we open ourselves to healthier relationships, deeper fulfillment, and lasting personal success.

My hope is that the next time your attitude starts drifting, you'll remember this chapter and breathe before reacting. That moment of recognition is not small—it is transformation in motion. Congratulations in advance: you are becoming more self-aware.

Attitude Storytime

There was a season in my life when I found myself frowning more often than smiling. Everything irritated me. My overall disposition was negative—especially toward my husband. What's interesting is that I seemed perfectly fine with everyone else. I couldn't identify the source of my frustration, but it was affecting my mood, my marriage, and my peace.

Both my husband and I came into our marriage with full lives behind us. We each had been married before. We share three wonderful adult children and four grandchildren. But my journey was marked by deep trauma—childhood physical abuse, sexual abuse, abandonment, and memories that followed me into adulthood. Even though we intentionally invited God into our relationship before getting married, and even though I felt ready and eager for this new commitment, I did not fully understand how much healing I still needed.

At first, everything was beautiful. We were connected, aligned, and excited for our future. But slowly, something shifted in me. I couldn't find peace. I went from calm to overwhelmed in an instant—not literally over spilled milk, but close enough. Confused, I turned to prayer, asking God to reveal what was truly happening beneath the surface.

And then the truth unfolded: I wasn't dealing with just one relationship stressor—I was caught in four. Unrealistic expectations. Trauma and past experiences. Lack of communication. Unresolved conflict. Attitude wasn't the only issue, but it magnified every one of them. My trauma had shaped expectations I didn't recognize. My assumptions clouded my judgment. My need for resolution fed my anxiety.

I've always been the type to either fix something immediately or flee from it altogether. Because I wanted so badly to resolve everything, I kept seeking solutions—but the harder I pushed, the more overwhelmed I felt.

In prayer, God invited me to shift my focus. Instead of examining my husband under a magnifying glass, the Holy Spirit instructed me to turn inward. To be still. To pause before I reacted. That simple shift changed everything. Through reflection, journaling, open conversations, and intentional growth, I began to understand my triggers and release attitudes that weren't serving me—or my marriage.

Now, when my attitude begins to drift, either I notice it or my husband does. We've set goals together, and he knows how to support me in ways that align with my healing. Journaling helps me separate the present from the past. Communication helps us stay connected. And prayer keeps me anchored.

At the end of the day, only one person can change your attitude—and that's you. Attitude is the number one relationship killer. I wish someone had told me sooner that my attitude alone had the power to make or break my connections.

What Research Says About a Positive Attitude

Before closing this chapter, I want to highlight what current research reveals about maintaining a positive attitude. Throughout this chapter, we've explored self-awareness, intentional growth, and the power of attitude in shaping relationships. But attitude doesn't just influence our communication or emotional patterns—it directly impacts our physical, mental, and spiritual well-being.

A positive attitude is far more than a pleasant disposition. It is a protective factor. It strengthens the body, steadies the mind, and nourishes the spirit. When we choose to interpret challenges with optimism, faith, or gratitude, our entire physiology responds. From decreased stress hormones to improved immunity, the benefits are both measurable and profound.

Reduced Stress and Stronger Immunity

Research consistently shows that a positive mindset helps regulate the body's stress response by reducing cortisol levels. Chronic stress elevates inflammation and puts strain on the immune system. Optimistic individuals, however, tend to experience fewer stress-related symptoms and recover more efficiently when illness does occur.

Cohen and Pressman (2006) found that people who practiced positive thinking displayed a stronger immune response to common viruses than those who approached life with negativity or fear. In many ways, optimism acts as a biological defense mechanism, helping the body restore balance during difficult seasons.

Cardiovascular Health

Heart health is also closely tied to attitude. Studies reveal that individuals who maintain a hopeful, positive outlook have lower blood pressure, reduced risk of heart disease, and healthier coping behaviors overall. Boehm and Kubzansky (2012) note that people with optimistic attitudes engage less in harmful stress-related behaviors such as emotional eating or smoking. When we cultivate peace within, our heart—physically and emotionally—benefits.

Enhanced Mental Resilience

A positive attitude builds mental resilience. It helps us adapt to challenges, recover from adversity, and maintain perspective when life feels overwhelming. Instead of focusing solely on loss or hardship, optimistic individuals look for meaning, purpose, or opportunity. This mindset reduces anxiety and depression by shifting attention from fear to possibility. Carver, Scheier, and Segerstrom (2010) found that optimism fosters higher levels of psychological well-being and problem-solving.

Longevity and Quality of Life

Perhaps one of the most striking findings in attitude research is its link to longevity. A Harvard study revealed that individuals with an optimistic outlook lived significantly longer than those with a pessimistic view—even when controlling for other health factors (Lee et al., 2019). Positivity does not erase pain or hardship, but it guides how we move through it. A hopeful heart sustains the body.

Improved Relationships and Social Health

Positive attitudes foster healthy social connection. People who consistently demonstrate gratitude, empathy, and encouragement tend to build stronger support networks—relationships that protect against loneliness, increase emotional health, and create a sense of belonging. Joy and compassion are emotionally contagious. When we uplift others, we also uplift ourselves.

Living It Out

A positive attitude does not eliminate hardship. It reframes it. Whether through prayer, reflection, journaling, time in nature, or intentional stillness, we can reset our mindset each day. The body follows where the mind leads—and the spirit strengthens them both. Choosing positivity is not denial; it is choosing health, clarity, and peace in the midst of real life.

Below, you'll find a worksheet designed to support your growth journey—one that helps you reflect on your attitude in intimate relationships, at work, and in friendships. Self-awareness and intentionality take courage, but this is your personal space to explore at your own pace. Share your reflections only when you feel ready. These exercises are not about perfection but about honest growth.

Pause & Reflect: A Check-In with Your Attitude

Before turning the page, take a quiet moment to pause and reflect. Growth does not begin in movement—it begins in stillness. When we slow down, we can finally hear what our heart, body, and mind have been trying to tell us. Use the prompts below for journaling, prayer, or personal reflection.

Self-Reflection Prompts

When do I feel most "out of alignment"?
Consider the moments, people, or patterns that drain your peace or shift your attitude. What do those situations reveal about your internal world?

What restores me?
Identify the activities, places, or spiritual practices that make you feel whole, centered, and renewed. How consistently do you make room for them?

What messages do I communicate through my attitude?
Even without speaking, your tone, energy, and presence send messages to your spouse, children, friends, and coworkers. What messages might they be receiving?

How does my attitude affect my physical health?
Notice the connection between your thoughts and your body. Stress and negativity often appear in your energy levels, sleep patterns, or motivation.

Where can I invite more gratitude or faith?
What is one small mindset shift you can make today that brings more hope, joy, or compassion into your life?

Pause & Reflect: Your Attitude at Work

The workplace exposes our attitudes more than we realize. Here, our patience is tested, our resilience is shaped, and our communication is sharpened. Reflect on how your mindset influences your workday, your peace, and your relationships on the job.

Self-Reflection Questions

Awareness & Mindset

- What attitude do I typically bring into the workday—hopeful, hurried, anxious, exhausted, or calm?
- How do I respond to unexpected challenges or interruptions?
- Do I notice mood patterns throughout the week? What might those patterns reveal about my work-life balance?
- How does my self-talk impact my confidence or motivation?
- When I make a mistake, do I see it as failure or as a lesson?

Relationships & Leadership

- How do I show respect and appreciation to colleagues, regardless of role or personality differences?
- Do I listen to understand, or do I listen to respond?
- In conflict, am I more committed to being right or to building understanding?
- What is one small way I can lighten someone else's load this week?
- How do I model grace, integrity, and emotional maturity—especially when no one is watching?

Growth & Intentionality

- Which attitudes or habits no longer serve me, and what new ones could I adopt?
- Do I celebrate progress, or do I only see what still needs improvement?
- How open am I to receiving feedback?
- When under stress, do I pause and reset or simply push through?
- What does "working with purpose" truly mean to me?

General Tips to Maintain a Healthy Attitude in All Relationships

Maintaining a healthy attitude requires ongoing intentionality. Regular self-reflection helps identify patterns before they become ingrained. Practicing mindfulness creates space between emotion and reaction, reducing impulsive responses. Staying open to change enables us to adapt rather than resist. Investing in personal growth strengthens emotional regulation and boosts confidence. And when deeply rooted attitudes require additional support, seeking guidance from a therapist, counselor, or pastor can lead to meaningful breakthroughs.

The healthier and more balanced we are individually, the healthier our relationships become.

After attitude comes assumptions—the quiet narratives we accept as truth until we slow down, ask, and replace guesses with understanding. In Chapter Two, we explored the harmful impact that unchecked assumptions can have in relationships. We used the relationship stressors to help frame how assumptions are one of the silent killers of connection. Assumptions can be seemingly innocent conclusions or beliefs—based on past experiences, incomplete information, or stereotypes. They can sneak into the way we interact with others, clouding our judgment and creating friction where none needs to exist.

Chapter 5: Assumptions *The Unspoken Stories We Tell Ourselves*

Assumptions are among the most dangerous forces in any relationship because they work quietly and internally. They form beneath conscious awareness—often before logic, communication, or emotional regulation have time to engage. As we explored in Chapter 2, the human brain is constantly scanning for safety, certainty, and belonging, shaping our perceptions long before we consciously interpret events. In this way, assumptions become automatic narratives—stories our nervous system tells to protect us from potential threat, rejection, or loss. Before we realize it, these narratives begin shaping how we interpret someone else's tone, behavior, or intentions.

In this chapter, we'll take a deeper look at why assumptions harm relationships so profoundly, what research reveals about their psychological impact, and how we can begin to break the cycle of assumption-based conflict.

What Are Assumptions?

At their core, assumptions are mental shortcuts—rapid conclusions our minds create to make sense of incomplete information. Neuroscience and trauma psychology confirm that these shortcuts often originate not from logic, but from emotional memory, survival instinct, and past experience. They allow us to respond quickly when our brains perceive uncertainty, stress, or emotional vulnerability.

Our assumptions are built on past experiences, emotional memory, cultural conditioning, fears, biases, and sometimes simple misunderstandings. As discussed in

Chapter 2, the brain's survival systems often prioritize protection over accuracy, meaning we are more likely to assume threat, rejection, or negative intent than safety or neutrality—especially when unresolved trauma is present.

While assumptions can occasionally be helpful—particularly when grounded in established trust—they often become harmful when they're rooted in insecurity, emotional wounds, or incomplete facts. In these moments, assumptions stop being tools of efficiency and start becoming barriers to truth, intimacy, and connection.

The Dangers of Assumptions: What Research Says

When assumptions go unexamined, they quietly undermine relationships. They distort communication, erode trust, and create emotional distance between people who may still care deeply for one another. Many assumptions begin with good intentions—trying to interpret someone's feelings, avoid conflict, or anticipate needs—but without clarification, these guesses often spiral into misinterpretations.

Communication breakdown is one of the earliest symptoms. When we assume we already know what someone thinks or feels, we stop asking questions. We stop listening. We begin reacting not to the person in front of us, but to the emotional narrative shaped by our internal filters—what Chapter 2 identified as the powerful interaction between attitude, assumptions, and expectations.

For example, if your partner comes home quiet and withdrawn after a long day, you might assume they're upset with you. This triggers defensiveness or emotional distance. In reality, they may simply be exhausted. This is how unconscious assumptions activate emotional responses that escalate conflict unnecessarily. Gottman and Silver

(1999) found that couples who make emotional assumptions without verifying them tend to remain stuck in unresolved conflict and dissatisfaction.

Assumptions also weaken trust. When we assume negative intent—especially without evidence—we begin to question another person's care, commitment, or character. Over time, this erodes emotional safety and connection.

In workplace settings, assumptions are equally destructive. If a colleague doesn't respond quickly to an email and you assume they're ignoring you, frustration and resentment form. Bradbury and Karney (2004) show that negative assumptions about others' intentions often lead to escalating tension and reduced trust across professional relationships.

A major danger of assumptions is their link to **negative attribution**—the belief that someone's behavior reflects who they are rather than what they're experiencing. Attribution Theory (Heider, 1958) explains that humans instinctively assign internal motives to others' actions. Bradbury and Fincham (1990) found that partners frequently blame each other personally instead of considering situational stressors—reinforcing emotional cycles that fuel resentment and distance.

Assumptions also promote **avoidance**. When someone assumes they are unwanted, unvalued, or unheard, emotional withdrawal begins. This withdrawal often triggers confusion and frustration in the other person, creating the demand-withdraw cycle described by Gottman (1994).

Finally, assumptions breed **resentment**. Unspoken beliefs—especially those grounded in misinterpretation—accumulate into emotional fatigue and bitterness. Berscheid et al. (1989) note that unresolved assumptions contribute significantly to long-term dissatisfaction in both personal and professional relationships.

Assumptions in Different Areas of Life

Assumptions operate across every domain of connection—romantic, familial, social, and professional. As outlined in Chapter 2, assumptions often develop automatically in moments of emotional uncertainty, particularly when stress, trauma, or unmet expectations are present.

Assumptions in Personal Life (Romantic and Intimate Relationships)

Our closest relationships carry the greatest emotional weight. Because of this, we often believe our partner *should just know* what we feel or need. But love does not equal mind reading.

Example 1: Expecting support without communicating the need.
You assume your partner can see your emotional distress. When support doesn't come, disappointment sets in. Canary and Dindia (2013) found that relationship satisfaction declines significantly when needs are assumed rather than communicated.

Example 2: Interpreting distraction as disinterest.
A stressed partner becomes emotionally distant. You assume loss of care. Gottman and Silver (1999) identify this pattern as a major contributor to emotional disengagement and conflict cycles.

Assumptions in the Workplace

Work environments amplify assumptions due to communication gaps, hierarchy, stress, and limited emotional context.

Example 1: Assuming avoidance.
Delayed responses are interpreted as disrespect. Hinds and Mortensen (2005) found this leads to increased workplace conflict.

Example 2: Assuming rejection.
Believing your ideas won't matter silences your voice. Morrison (2011) shows this reduces innovation and professional growth.

Assumptions in Friendships

Friendships depend on emotional safety, yet assumptions quietly fracture connection.

Example 1: Assuming unavailability.
You retreat emotionally without checking in. McNally et al. (2014) found this weakens emotional support.

Example 2: Assuming emotional awareness.
Silence replaces clarity. Ruus (2011) links this to increased relational distance.

Conclusion: Why Assumptions Are Harmful

Assumptions block truth. They distort perception, hinder communication, and create emotional separation. As Chapter 2 demonstrated, assumptions function beneath conscious awareness, driven by emotional memory and survival response rather than present reality.

Assumptions isolate. Curiosity reconnects.
Assumptions divide. Communication heals.

The moment we question our assumptions, their power weakens. When curiosity replaces fear, and clarity replaces silence, relationships begin to heal.

Assumption Storytime: When Assumptions Become Armor

I mentioned earlier that assumptions can create some of the loneliest seasons of our lives—and I know that truth firsthand. When you grow up carrying intersectional trauma, your nervous system learns to expect danger before safety, disappointment before joy. This aligns directly with what Chapter 2 revealed: unresolved trauma shapes our unconscious assumptions long before logic has a chance to intervene.

Sexual abuse. Domestic violence. Racism. Abandonment. Discrimination. Emotional abuse. Each trauma layered another protective story inside me.

I developed emotional armor and called it strength.

My "superwoman disposition" masked isolation. It looked like resilience but functioned as self-protection. I assumed disappointment was inevitable. I assumed relationships would end. I assumed independence was survival.

But eventually, I realized:

My assumptions were protecting me from connection.

They kept me safe—but they also kept me from love.

Healing required conscious awareness, reflection, prayer, and intentional growth. As I challenged my assumptions, connection slowly replaced fear. I learned that assumptions may help us survive, but truth is what allows us to finally live.

Pause & Reflect: Checking Your Assumptions

As we learned in Chapter 2, assumptions often operate beneath conscious awareness. This reflection brings them into the light—where healing begins.

Self-Reflection Prompts: Personal Relationships

• When was the last time I assumed someone should know what I needed?
• How did that assumption impact connection?
• What emotional memories might be influencing my interpretations?
• How often do I verify rather than assume?
• What assumption can I release today?

Pause & Reflect: Assumptions at Work

Awareness & Mindset

• What story do I tell myself when communication is unclear?
• How do stress and fatigue influence my interpretations?
• Do I assume others understand my workload or emotional state?
• What one shift can replace assumption with curiosity?

Collaboration & Leadership

• How do I respond when assumptions are challenged?
• How can I create more psychological safety for others

Pause & Reflect: Friendships

• Do I assume my friends know how I feel?
• Do I retreat instead of clarify?
• What fears drive my assumptions?
• How can I choose grace over presumption?

General Reflection: From Assumption to Awareness

• What patterns appear across my assumptions?
• How does stress influence my interpretations?
• What would shift if I replaced assumptions with questions?
• How can prayer, reflection, or mindfulness support emotional regulation?

Living It Out

Assumptions lose power when examined. This week, pause before filling in the blanks. Ask. Clarify. Extend grace.

"Everyone should be quick to listen, slow to speak, and slow to become angry." — James 1:19

This verse beautifully captures relational maturity. It aligns perfectly with what neuroscience and emotional intelligence teach: when we slow down, regulate our reactions, and remain curious, we create emotional safety.

Every time you pause, ask, and listen—you dismantle assumption.
Every time you seek understanding—you rebuild trust.

Assumptions isolate.
Truth reconnects.

Chapter 6: Expectations in Relationships– *How Invisible Demands Shape Emotional Safety and Trust*

We have explored attitude—how we show up—and assumptions—the stories we create without checking them. Now we turn to the third and final root of relational breakdown: expectations. Not the healthy, shared, mutually understood ones, but the silent, rigid, or unrealistic expectations that quietly shape the way we interpret the world and the people in it.

This chapter isn't calling you to abandon standards or boundaries. Instead, it invites you to exchange hidden expectations for clear, shared agreements—the kind that build trust instead of tension, clarity instead of confusion, connection instead of disappointment. And as we established in Chapter 2, many of our expectations don't begin as conscious decisions—they form through emotional memory, lived experience, cultural conditioning, and the nervous system's ongoing drive for safety, predictability, and control. When expectations are unspoken, they don't just create frustration; they activate threat responses, intensify stress reactions, and quietly erode emotional safety.

The Silent Killer of Connection: What Research Says About Expectations

Expectations can be the silent killer of any relationship. They linger like an uninvited guest—present, invisible, and waiting for the right moment to sabotage connection. The issue is not that we have expectations; humans naturally form them. The issue is that our expectations are often unspoken, unreasonable, or rigid, shaped by past experiences, cultural norms, personal values, or emotional history. As Chapter 2 highlighted, when stress is high or emotional capacity is low, our brains tend to default to "shoulds" as a form of stability—attempting to create certainty in uncertain moments. But that internal push for certainty can easily become a relational pressure point.

Left unexpressed, expectations breed disappointment and resentment. Whether in the workplace, at home, or among friends, uncommunicated desires create a recipe for misunderstanding and frustration. Research consistently shows that mismatched expectations are among the leading predictors of relational dissatisfaction (Gottman & Silver, 1999). Thankfully, the solution isn't to eliminate all expectations—it's to release the silent ones and replace them with honesty, clarity, and compassion.

Unrealistic Expectations in the Workplace

The workplace is often a breeding ground for unrealistic expectations. Leaders may assign goals that appear reasonable on paper but fail to clarify what support or resources are actually available. Employees, in turn, may pressure themselves to overperform—taking on too much, too fast, without asking for help. These unrealistic pressures create burnout, emotional fatigue, and resentment that ripple through teams. And as Chapter 2 emphasized, chronic stress reduces emotional regulation and shrinks our relational bandwidth—making it harder to communicate needs, ask clarifying questions, or interpret others with generosity.

We must also be mindful of what we expect from others when we personally understand the weight of a task. Familiarity with the burden should produce empathy—not unrealistic demands.

Healthy professional relationships thrive when people communicate openly, set realistic boundaries, and take ownership of their share of the workload. Professional relationships at their best are collaborative and equitable. One of the hardest truths to accept is that everyone operates on a different playing field. Two people may share the same task, but because no two individuals are alike, their capacities, challenges, and circumstances will always differ. Chapter 2 reinforced this reality: the same stressor does not impact every nervous system the same way, and expectations must account for human variability—not idealized performance.

It becomes the employer's responsibility to ensure expectations are clear, consistent, and tailored when appropriate. That is simply the world we live in now.

Unclear expectations are equally toxic. When roles and responsibilities aren't defined, people assume others will fill in the gaps. Projects stall, communication breaks down, and trust erodes. A workplace built on guessing and resentment cannot survive. Research by Eisenberg et al. (2019) confirms that ambiguous expectations significantly increase workplace conflict and role confusion.

The antidote is clarity—speaking up, asking questions, confirming understanding, and ensuring everyone knows what is expected, what is available, and what is realistically possible.

Silos and the Overloaded Leader

Some organizations operate in deep silos—isolated teams relying on one leader to be the sole communicator, problem-solver, and emotional buffer. Employees begin expecting their manager to resolve every issue, meet every need, and anticipate every concern. When expectations pile up in this way, collaboration collapses. And when one person becomes the emotional container for an entire system, the stress response escalates—not only for the leader, but for the team. As Chapter 2 made clear, high stress environments amplify irritation, misinterpretation, and emotional reactivity, creating a workplace culture where resentment replaces responsibility.

Managers burn out under the weight of unrealistic responsibility. Team members become frustrated when unspoken needs go unmet. Everyone suffers.

Breaking this cycle requires shared ownership—a shift from "They should fix it" to "Here's what I need, and here's what I can contribute." It is a movement toward teamwork rather than dependency, empowerment rather than expectation.

Unspoken Rules in Romantic and Family Relationships

Romantic and family relationships carry some of the heaviest unspoken expectations. We carry silent beliefs about how others should respond, care, communicate, or behave—beliefs shaped by upbringing, trauma, prior partners, and cultural norms. And as Chapter 2 emphasized, when trauma or chronic stress is present, expectations can become a nervous-system strategy—an attempt to prevent disappointment by controlling outcomes. But relationships cannot thrive under pressure to perform or mind-read.

Hidden expectations sound like: you should know what I need without me saying it; you should handle conflict the way I do; you should always—or never—react a certain way. These invisible "should" quietly chip away at intimacy.

Love is not mind-reading. Love is communication.

Healthy families and couples exchange assumptions for agreements—clear commitments that protect emotional safety. An agreement might be pausing ten minutes before discussing a conflict, scheduling one tech-free dinner per week, or letting each other know when space is needed so silence isn't misinterpreted as rejection. This aligns with Chapter 2's emphasis on emotional regulation: when people create shared agreements, they reduce uncertainty—and uncertainty is one of the fastest triggers for relational stress responses.

Spoken needs lose their power to wound and gain the power to unite.

Friendships and the Weight of Assumed Support

Friendships often fall victim to assumed availability. We expect friends to always answer, always show up, always understand our tone or emotional state without explanation. When they don't, disappointment takes root, even though the unmet expectation was never voiced. And as discussed in Chapter 2, when people are overloaded, tired, grieving, or stressed, their relational capacity shifts—even if their care does not. Expectations that ignore capacity create unnecessary hurt.

Instead of withdrawing, we can initiate honest questions such as: "Hey, is everything okay between us?" or "I miss you—can we plan some time together?" Healthy friendships allow honesty, imperfection, and grace. When we release expectations, we make room for empathy.

Replacing Expectations with Responsibility

A turning point in emotional maturity is recognizing that freedom begins when we take ownership of our needs. Instead of waiting for others to meet unspoken desires, we communicate openly. This aligns with Chapter 2's internal-work theme: responsibility is one of the most stabilizing forces in relationships because it moves us from emotional guessing to emotional clarity. Research supports this shift—clear communication and shared expectations predict higher relational satisfaction across all relationship types (Overall & McNulty, 2017).

When we take responsibility for what we feel, need, and value, we empower ourselves and those we love.

This shift transforms every kind of relationship. Communication becomes clearer because guessing games disappear. Conflict decreases because misunderstandings have nowhere to hide. Trust deepens as honesty replaces hidden rules. Collaboration replaces codependence because responsibility is shared rather than assumed. Burnout fades because the emotional and practical labor is distributed evenly. And as Chapter 2 emphasized, when the emotional load is shared, nervous systems settle—making connection easier to sustain.

When this shift occurs, relationships stop feeling heavy—they begin to feel aligned.

The Power of Shared Agreements

The strongest relationships whether personal or professional—operate on shared agreements, not silent expectations. Shared agreements are born from dialogue, mutual respect, and emotional honesty. They are not rules forced on someone; they are commitments formed collaboratively. And psychologically, they reduce ambiguity—one of the most common triggers of stress, insecurity, and relational reactivity identified in Chapter 2.

An agreement might be checking in weekly, discussing concerns before assuming the worst, or clearly communicating when quiet time is needed. These small agreements create structure, peace, and emotional safety. They eliminate guessing, reduce tension, and strengthen trust.

In a world full of unspoken expectations, shared agreements are anchors.

Conclusion: Communication Is the Cure

When we release hidden expectations and replace them with communication, understanding grows. When we take responsibility for our needs, resentment shrinks. And when we create agreements instead of assumptions, our relationships—personal and professional—become places of peace rather than pressure.

So yes—throw out the silent expectations. They're too heavy to carry and too inconsistent to sustain. Trade them for dialogue, compassion, and shared responsibility. What remains isn't emptiness—it's genuine connection.

Walking Together in Agreement

Do two walk together unless they have agreed to do so?
— *Amos 3:3 (NIV)*

Unity cannot exist without agreement. Two people cannot walk forward together unless they share an understanding of where they're going and how they'll travel. When expectations are unclear, relationships move out of sync—pulling in different directions and creating tension where there should be peace. And as Chapter 2 reinforced, tension grows when uncertainty grows—because the human mind tries to fill unclear space with pressure, control, or storylines.

Amos 3:3 invites us to pause and ask: Have we truly agreed on how we're walking together?

Agreement is not about sameness. It is about shared purpose and the grace to adjust when needed. When we create space for honest dialogue and shared agreements, we walk in step—not because life is perfect, but because our hearts are aligned.

Walking in agreement mirrors how God walks with us. He doesn't force alignment; He invites it. He communicates through His Word, His Spirit, and His love. Clarity builds connection. When we release hidden expectations and choose communication, we practice divine partnership—walking intentionally, patiently, and with love guiding every step.

Pause & Reflect — Expectations at Work

Take a moment to consider how expectations—spoken or unspoken—shape your experience in the workplace. Reflect on where clarity is needed, where frustration may be rooted in silence, and where collaboration could grow through honest dialogue.

Ask yourself:
• What expectations have I placed on colleagues or supervisors without actually expressing them?
• How do unclear goals or unspoken assumptions affect my communication, motivation, or confidence?
• In what ways can I turn my private expectations into shared, collaborative agreements?
• How might open dialogue reduce frustration or burnout within my team?
• What is one professional expectation I can clarify this week to strengthen connection or productivity?

Pause & Reflect — Expectations in Intimate & Family Relationships

Silent expectations run deepest in the relationships that matter most. This reflection invites honesty—with yourself and with those you love.

Consider:
• When have I expected a partner or family member to "just know" what I needed?
• How often do I express my needs before resentment begins to build?
• Which unspoken rules in my relationships need to be voiced, revised, or released?
• How can I invite more grace and curiosity when expectations aren't met?
• What would it look like to replace a hidden "should" with a simple, honest agreement?

Pause & Reflect — Expectations in Friendships & General Relationships

Friendships require spaciousness—space for changing seasons, evolving needs, and human imperfection.

Expectations often shrink that space. And as Chapter 2 emphasized, when stress is high, we tend to interpret "less access" as "less care," even when it isn't.

Reflect on the following:
• How do my expectations shape the way I relate to friends and daily interactions?
• What patterns of disappointment repeat because I haven't communicated my needs?
• How can I practice assuming less and asking more?
• Where might I be holding people to standards I never actually shared with them?
• What peace might I experience by letting go of just one unrealistic expectation today?

Living It Out — The Work Within

Before we show up well for others—romantically, professionally, or within our families—we must examine how we show up for ourselves. Expectations begin internally. They are shaped by our self-esteem, our emotional wounds, our sense of worthiness, and the beliefs we carry about what love, loyalty, or partnership should look like. And as Chapter 2 established, when the inner world is dysregulated—when stress, trauma, or emotional fatigue are running the system—expectations often become rigid, reactive, or controlling, not because we're "too much," but because our nervous system is trying to feel safe.

The health of every relationship begins with the health of the individual.

If your inner world is filled with fear, insecurity, or unhealed trauma, those dynamics will quietly seep into every friendship, marriage, or team you join. Before walking with others in peace, you must learn to walk with yourself in wholeness. When you create clarity within, you naturally begin to create clarity around you. When you regulate internally, you relate differently externally. And that is where expectations transform—from silent pressure into shared partnership.

Chapter 7: The First Relationship — *You*

Every relationship we form mirrors our internal world. The way we love, trust, communicate, and even argue reflects our emotional health—or the places still seeking healing. Long before we learn communication skills or relationship strategies, our nervous system learns how to survive, attach, and protect itself. As we explored in Chapter 2, neuroscience and trauma psychology confirm that our brains are constantly scanning for safety, certainty, and belonging, shaping how we show up in connection.

This chapter is not about perfection; it is about awareness. It is about doing the inner work required to heal what is wounded, nurture what is beautiful, and strengthen what is still growing. For many, this may be the hardest chapter to read—because it asks you to look inward with honesty and courage.

Healthy relationships don't happen simply because two people care. They flourish when both people commit to emotional growth. Emotional maturity is not a destination; it is a discipline. It requires us to pause, reflect, and take ownership of our triggers, fears, nervous system responses, and relational patterns before they become someone else's burden.

And now, here comes the hard work.

Looking Back to Look Forward

Sit quietly for a moment and think about your life. Truly think. How was your childhood? Were both parents present, or did you grow up in a home fractured by silence, conflict, emotional distance, or absence? And look deeper—how was *their* childhood? Because what they inherited is often what they passed down.

Family systems theory (Bowen, 1978) tells us that emotional patterns echo through generations, shaping how we connect, cope, regulate emotion, and communicate. Many of us promised ourselves we would "do better" than what we experienced—and in many ways, we have. But neuroscience reminds us that the emotional blueprint of our past becomes embedded in our nervous system, influencing our responses unless we consciously bring it into awareness and begin to rewrite it.

There's an old saying: *"Hurt people hurt people."* I would take it further—broken people often raise broken people. But the story does not end there. Healing begins the moment awareness enters the room.

Ask yourself: Was your childhood home filled with laughter or with tension—or both? Whatever emotional tone dominated your environment likely settled deepest into your nervous system. Were words of love spoken freely, or was affection something you had to interpret through subtle gestures? Were conflicts loud and unpredictable, or were they silently avoided?

These patterns matter. They teach us what to expect from love, safety, and connection.

Attachment theory (Bowlby, 1988; Ainsworth, 1989) shows that our early experiences form our attachment style, influencing how we trust, seek closeness, regulate distress, and handle conflict in adulthood. If chaos, neglect, or emotional unpredictability defined your early years, emotional safety may now feel foreign—or even threatening.

And pain doesn't always originate from the home as a structure. Often, it emerges from what happened inside or outside those walls—sometimes at the hands of those who were meant to protect us.

My Story: Trauma, Survival, and Awakening

Part of my story looks like this:

I was molested as a child—by people who were supposed to care for me. That experience created deep confusion about my body, my worth, and what love even meant. As a child and young woman, trust felt dangerous. Vulnerability felt unsafe.

That wound followed me into adulthood, layered with additional trauma: witnessing domestic violence in my home, then finding myself in relationships where domestic violence reappeared. Trauma stacked upon trauma, eventually forming what psychologists refer to as complex PTSD (Herman, 1992). I describe it as flight syndrome—when things became emotionally intense, I fled. Leaving felt safer than staying. Distance felt safer than vulnerability.

Trauma research confirms this survival pattern. Early abuse and repeated exposure to violence dysregulate the nervous system, priming the brain for hypervigilance, avoidance, emotional numbing, and chronic fear (van der Kolk, 2014). When the body learns danger before it learns safety, survival becomes the default response.

To show up fully in my marriage today, I had to choose intentional healing—so my husband could receive the healthiest version of me. Not the perfect version, but the healing one. Because not only does he deserve that—I deserve it too.

This is the heart of this chapter: **healthy relationships grow when both people commit to healing.**

Honest Questions for the Journey

Here are some hard—but necessary—questions to ask yourself:

- How did divorce affect you as a child, if that was part of your story? Research on attachment disruption (Amato, 2000) shows that children of divorce often carry heightened anxiety around rejection and abandonment into adulthood.
- How did losing a parent or caregiver shape your relationship with loss today? Studies on grief and attachment (Bowlby, 1980) demonstrate that early loss creates lifelong sensitivity to separation.
- Do you repeat emotional patterns you swore you would never repeat—choosing emotionally unavailable partners, tolerating disrespect, staying silent when you feel unsafe? This phenomenon, known as repetition compulsion (Freud, 1920/1958), explains how we unconsciously recreate familiar pain, hoping for different outcomes.

This is not about shame.

It is about awakening.

If you need a moment to breathe, take it. You are not falling apart—you are waking up. And awakening is the beginning of healing.

You are not weak for needing healing. You are wise for seeking it.

Carl Rogers (1961) believed that genuine relationships grow in an atmosphere of congruence—when our inner reality matches our outer expression. Emotional health creates that alignment. It allows us to show up fully, honestly, and without the protective masks we learned to wear.

Your emotional health is the ground beneath your feet. Without it, even the purest love will stumble. With it, every relationship gains the opportunity to deepen in trust, safety, and intimacy.

Healing as a Daily Practice

Emotional health is not a one-time achievement; it is a daily decision. Healing happens in small, intentional moments—pausing before reacting, noticing emotional triggers, soothing the nervous system, choosing reflection over defense.

As healing unfolds, our **attitude softens from defensiveness to openness**. Our **assumptions shift from suspicion to curiosity**. Our **expectations evolve from rigid demands to shared understanding**. Healing transforms survival into connection—and connection into trust.

You cannot change your past, but you can change how it lives inside your body, your mind, and your spirit. Every moment you choose awareness over avoidance, truth over denial, forgiveness over bitterness, and regulation over reactivity, you reclaim a piece of yourself.

Healing yourself is not selfish—it is sacred. When you heal, you become a safe place for others to heal too.

Pause & Reflect — Healing Beyond the Home

Use these prompts to explore your emotional readiness for healthy connection. Reflect, write, pray, or simply breathe with each one.

Self-Awareness

What emotions from your past still influence how you react today?
When threatened, do you fight, flee, freeze, or fawn?
How do you speak to yourself when you are hurting—gently or harshly?

Attitude Check

How does your attitude toward others reflect how you feel about yourself?
When disappointed, do you respond with patience or punishment?
What practices help regulate your emotions and restore balance?

Challenging Assumptions

What stories do you tell yourself in moments of uncertainty—and where did those stories begin?
How often do you question your thoughts before reacting?
What assumptions about love, safety, or loyalty need rewriting?

Examining Expectations

What unspoken expectations do you place on others—and are they fair?
Do you voice your needs or hope people will "just know"?
What hidden expectation can you turn into a shared agreement this week?

Commitment to Heal

Who do you need to forgive—yourself, a parent, a partner?
What does emotional wholeness look like for you?
How will you know you are growing?

Living It Out

Healing is the act of guarding your heart—not by building walls, but by cultivating wisdom, self-awareness, and compassion.

Because when your heart is whole, every relationship—personal, professional, or spiritual—has room to flourish.

Transition: From Healing to Companionship

Once you begin tending to your inner world—regulating your emotions, softening your attitude, challenging your assumptions, and releasing unrealistic expectations—you open the door to genuine companionship.

Healing prepares you to love without losing yourself.
To connect without control.
To walk beside others with grace, steadiness, and strength.

Get ready to reclaim **the journey.**

Chapter 8: Reclaiming the Journey of Life; in Companionship

True companionship—whether in marriage, friendship, or community—requires two people who are not looking to be completed but to be complemented. Emotional health gives us the ability to bring our wholeness into connection and say, *"Let's grow together."*

As we explored in Chapter 2, our nervous systems are constantly scanning for safety, belonging, and connection. When healing occurs, our internal world shifts—and so does the way we relate. Relationships move from survival to purpose, from chaos to clarity, from fear to freedom.

When you heal, companionship becomes a place of peace rather than pressure, security rather than uncertainty, and growth rather than fear.

Walking Together with Intention

Healthy companionship doesn't happen by accident; it happens by intention. It is the daily decision to show up—not only when life is easy, but especially when it is hard. It means communicating before frustration builds, apologizing before pride takes over, and listening even when you disagree.

You will know you are growing when your **attitude** shifts from *"What can I get from this person?"* to *"How can I understand and support them?"*
When your **assumptions** soften from *"They're against me"* to *"Maybe they're overwhelmed, hurting, or unsure."*
And when your **expectations** evolve from *"They should know"* to *"Let me clearly express what I need."*

This is the fruit of healing—emotional maturity that allows peace to replace panic, and patience to replace punishment.

Companionship does not erase conflict; it transforms how we navigate it. When both people are emotionally grounded, disagreement no longer feels like danger—it becomes an opportunity to deepen trust. You begin to realize that the goal isn't to win the argument; it is to preserve the connection.

The same principle applies in the workplace. Teams thrive when people bring emotional health to the table—when leaders model humility instead of hierarchy, when colleagues assume the best instead of the worst, and when expectations are communicated rather than guessed. Whether leading a department, managing a classroom, or collaborating on a project, emotional maturity is what separates a toxic workplace from a thriving one.

When you can engage with empathy, clarify expectations, and regulate your reactions, you elevate not only the relationship but the culture. Work becomes not just about tasks—but about trust.

When Love Meets Accountability

Healing also teaches us that love without accountability isn't love at all.

Healthy companionship means being gentle and honest at the same time. It is the ability to say, *"I love you enough to tell you the truth, even when it's uncomfortable."* Real love calls us higher. It does not enable harmful behavior, nor does it demand perfection. It invites both people into awareness, responsibility, and growth.

The same is true in leadership and professional relationships. Healthy workplaces are built on truth spoken in love. Accountability in teams means we value integrity over comfort. We can give feedback without fear and receive it without shame. When we separate correction from condemnation, we create safety, trust, and respect.

If one person in a relationship—or one member of a team—is committed to growth while the other resists it, imbalance will always follow. Companionship thrives when both are willing to look inward and ask, *"How am I contributing to the health or harm of this relationship?"*

That is emotional maturity.
That is healing in motion.

Friendship as the Foundation

We often limit the idea of companionship to romantic relationships, but friendship is just as vital. Every healthy marriage, partnership, or team begins with friendship—mutual respect, empathy, laughter, and trust.

A true friend is not the one who always agrees with you, but the one who sees your flaws and still chooses to stay. They tell you when you are wrong, but never stop believing in who you can become.

If you find friends who bring peace instead of pressure, clarity instead of confusion, and accountability instead of chaos—cherish them. They are gifts. And strive to be that friend for others. Be the safe space you once prayed for. Speak words that heal rather than harm.

Friendships rooted in honesty and grace become the blueprint for every other relationship we build—at home, at work, and in community.

The Power of Agreement

"Two are better than one… If either of them falls down, one can help the other up."
— **Ecclesiastes 4:9–10 (NIV)**
Walking together requires shared purpose and responsibility.

"As iron sharpens iron, so one person sharpens another."
— **Proverbs 27:17 (NIV)**
Implies intentional proximity and mutual alignment.

Agreement does not mean uniformity—it means unity. It means both people understand where they are going and how they will walk there.

In healed companionship, agreement is not forced—it is formed. It is born from dialogue, respect, and shared values. You learn to check in not to control, but to connect. In the workplace, this type of agreement creates alignment. Teams move forward when everyone understands the vision, respects each other's roles, and feels valued for their contribution.

When emotional intelligence guides collaboration, professional interaction becomes partnership.

When healing and humility lead the way, walking together in peace—whether at home or in your organization—becomes one of life's greatest privileges.

Reclaiming Joy in the Journey

Life was never meant to be walked alone. Even the strongest among us need someone who sees us, understands us, and reminds us who we are when life grows heavy.

Healing does not isolate us; it prepares us to walk with others in truth.

Reclaiming the journey of life in companionship means you no longer chase connection from emptiness. You no longer attach out of fear. You connect from abundance.

When you are whole, you give love freely—not to prove your worth, but to express it. You listen deeply, forgive quickly, and love courageously. You stop surviving relationships and start building them.

The same applies in the professional realm. Emotionally healthy people create emotionally healthy organizations. Leaders who have done the inner work cultivate psychological safety, where people feel free to speak, create, and grow without fear of ridicule or retaliation. Healthy companionship in the workplace looks like collaboration rooted in respect—where differences become strengths and feedback becomes fuel for growth.

That is what healing makes possible:
relationships that reflect peace,
friendships that mirror faith,
and work cultures shaped by honor, trust, and shared purpose.

Pause & Reflect — The Journey Toward Companionship

Healthy companionship does not happen by accident. It is a daily decision to show up—in ease and in difficulty. It means communicating before frustration builds, apologizing before pride hardens, and listening even in disagreement.

You know you are growing when:

- Your mindset shifts from *"What can I get?"* to *"How can I understand and support?"*
- Your assumptions soften from *"They're against me"* to *"They may be overwhelmed or hurting."*
- Your expectations shift from *"They should know"* to *"Let me clearly express what I need."*
- Conflict no longer signals danger—but becomes an invitation for deeper connection.

Chapter 9: Bringing It All Together — *The Relationship Stressors Revisited*

As we reach the final chapter of this journey, it's As we reach the final chapter of this journey, it's important to pause and recognize how far you've come. You've looked inward with honesty, examined your emotional patterns with courage, and reflected on your relationships with a level of depth many people never allow themselves to reach. You've explored your past, your pain, your resilience, and your healing. You've seen how your inner world—your nervous system, your emotional memory, your beliefs, and your lived experiences—shapes every relationship you touch.

This chapter ties everything together.

No matter how emotionally healthy, self-aware, or grounded you become, life will still test your growth. Stressors will still appear. Triggers will still surface. Old patterns may still knock. You will face one, two, or even several of the Relationship Stressors discussed earlier—sometimes all at once. But the difference now is simple and powerful: **you are equipped. You are aware. You are no longer navigating relationships blindly.**

Everything you've learned comes down to two core truths.

First, you now understand yourself more deeply through healing. You've explored your history, questioned your habits, and acknowledged your heart. You understand how your brain and nervous system learned to respond to threat, connection, conflict, and closeness. You recognize your triggers, your emotional reflexes, and your survival patterns. And most importantly, you now know how to pause, regulate, and choose response over reaction. Healing has given you language for your pain and tools for your growth.

Second, you understand the shaping power of **attitude, assumptions, and expectations.** These three—your posture, your internal narratives, and your silent rulebook—form the lens through which you interpret every interaction. Together, they determine whether a connection deepens or deteriorates, whether conflict heals or harms, and whether relationships become safe spaces or emotional battlegrounds.

When healing and awareness merge, something transformative happens: **you begin to experience freedom in relationships.** You may not always get it right—but now you notice sooner. You sense the emotional shift earlier. You recognize tension before it escalates, miscommunication before it fractures, and emotional distance before it hardens. Instead of spiraling, shutting down, or defending yourself, you now possess the ability to pause, reflect, and repair.

That pause becomes your power.

Before we close, let's revisit the eleven Relationship Stressors—this time through the lens of healing, emotional maturity, nervous system awareness, and restored connection:

- **Lack of Communication** becomes fertile ground for assumptions. When honest dialogue fades, the brain fills in the blanks—often with fear-based interpretations. Healing teaches us to slow down, ask questions, and listen with curiosity rather than defensiveness.

- **Dishonesty or Deception** reveals an underlying attitude problem rooted in fear, avoidance, or emotional self-protection. Healing restores integrity, helping us choose truth over comfort and connection over concealment.
- **Unresolved Conflict** reflects attitude and emotional regulation. When discomfort feels threatening, avoidance takes over. Healing reframes conflict as a pathway to understanding rather than a danger to escape.
- **Selfishness or Self-Centeredness** begins with attitude as well. When emotional survival eclipses emotional awareness, connection suffocates. Growth teaches reciprocity, empathy, and shared responsibility.
- **Jealousy and Insecurity** are shaped by assumptions formed through past wounds and emotional memory. Healing restores identity, emotional safety, and self-trust—quieting the urge to compare or compete.
- **Lack of Empathy** damages relationships when our nervous system shifts into self-protection instead of connection. Healing reopens emotional awareness and compassion, restoring our capacity to feel with others, not just react to them.
- **Toxic Behavior or Abuse** is rooted in destructive attitudes of control, domination, fear, and entitlement. Healing teaches boundaries, accountability, truth-telling, and the courage to pursue safety and peace.
- **Lack of Boundaries** emerges from unspoken expectations and emotional confusion. Healing empowers clarity, self-respect, and emotional responsibility—allowing limits to protect connection rather than threaten it.
- **Trauma or Past Experiences** shape the assumptions we carry about love, safety, and trust. Healing interrupts old emotional scripts, helping us

respond to present reality rather than relive past pain.

- **External Stressors**, such as finances, illness, leadership demands, or life transitions, test our emotional regulation and attitude under pressure. Awareness teaches us to link arms rather than point fingers.
- **Cultural or Value Differences** become stressful when interpreted through fear-based assumptions. Healing and humility allow curiosity to replace judgment, transforming difference into depth.

Each stressor reveals something about you—your emotional triggers, your nervous system patterns, your coping strategies, and your capacity for compassion. But now, you understand the roots beneath them. You recognize how **attitude shapes your posture, assumptions shape your interpretations, and expectations shape your emotional responses and communication.**

So, when conflict arises, disappointment surfaces, or emotional distance begins to form, you now possess a powerful internal compass. You pause and ask yourself:

- **What is my attitude in this moment—am I reacting or responding?**
- **What assumptions am I making without verifying?**
- **What expectations have I created that I haven't communicated?**

That pause is where your growth lives.
That pause is where healing does its work.
That pause is what preserves relationships.

Because when you understand yourself, you can finally understand others. And that is where real connection begins.

As you move forward into the relationships waiting for you—those you will build, those you will repair, and those you will release—carry this truth with you:

Healing is not the end of the journey. It is the beginning of deeper, healthier, more meaningful connection.

You are no longer walking blind.
You are walking empowered.
You are walking awake.

And for the first time, you are walking into relationships with the clarity, courage, emotional intelligence, and compassion you've always deserved.

You've reclaimed the journey.
Now go walk it—whole, healed, and connected.

Author's Final Note

If you've made it this far, I want to pause and simply say—thank you. Thank you for choosing honesty over avoidance, growth over comfort, and reflection over blame. You've done something sacred: you've faced yourself.

Writing this book wasn't easy. I didn't write from a mountaintop of mastery but from the middle of my own healing. Every chapter came from lived experience—moments of heartbreak, silence, disappointment, and revelation. I've known the exhaustion of trying to fix others while ignoring my own wounds, and the loneliness that comes from carrying unspoken pain.

But I've also known restoration—the kind that begins quietly, in the hidden corners of the soul, and whispers: "You can start again."

If this book has done anything for you, I hope it has reminded you of this truth: you are not broken beyond repair. You are becoming. Every mistake, every disappointment, and every healing step has shaped you into someone wiser, softer, and stronger. Someone capable of love that is both grounded and gracious.

Love—whether in marriage, friendship, family, or work—will always test your growth. It will stretch your patience, challenge your perspective, and reveal your deepest attitudes, assumptions, and expectations. But love is not about perfection; it is about practice. It's about showing up, even when it's hard, and choosing communication over confusion, curiosity over assumption, and grace over judgment.

Healing is the foundation of every healthy relationship. It helps you see others not through the lens of your pain, but through the eyes of compassion. When you understand yourself, you begin to understand others—and that's when real connection begins.

There is no finish line to this journey. Healing continues. Growth deepens. But the more you practice awareness, the freer your heart becomes—and the more peace you bring into every space you enter, whether that space is your home, your workplace, or your own thoughts.

So, as you close this book, I leave you with this truth: you are in control. You are not powerless to your past or to the patterns of others. You have the ability to shape your relationships, your peace, and your purpose—because it all begins with you.

Your attitude determines how you show up. Your assumptions determine how you interpret others. Your expectations determine how you communicate and connect.

When you lead with love, everything changes. So, keep showing up for yourself. Keep practicing the pause. Keep asking, listening, forgiving, and growing. Keep choosing peace when pride wants to win. And most importantly—keep choosing love. Yes, love your friends. Love your family. Love your partner. And yes, even love your coworkers. Because one of the greatest commandments reminds us to do just that:

"'Love the Lord your God with all your heart and with all your soul and with all your mind.' This is the first and greatest commandment.
And the second is like it: 'Love your neighbor as yourself.'"
— Matthew 22:37–39 (NIV)

I boldly tell you: choose love. Always.

With peace and gratitude,

Dr. Moni Kay
Author | Educator | Speaker | Believer in Healing

References

Ainsworth, M. D. S. (1989). Attachments beyond infancy. *American Psychologist, 44*(4), 709–716. https://doi.org/10.1037/0003-066X.44.4.709

Amato, P. R. (2000). The consequences of divorce for adults and children. *Journal of Marriage and Family, 62*(4), 1269–1287. https://doi.org/10.1111/j.1741-3737.2000.01269.x

Berscheid, E., Hatfield, E., & Walster, E. (1989). *Interpersonal attraction and romantic love*. Addison-Wesley.

Berscheid, E., Snyder, M., & Omoto, A. M. (1989). The relationship closeness inventory: Assessing the closeness of interpersonal relationships. *Journal of Personality and Social Psychology, 57*(5), 792–807. https://doi.org/10.1037/0022-3514.57.5.792

Boehm, J. K., & Kubzansky, L. D. (2012). The heart's content: The association between positive psychological well-being and cardiovascular health. *Psychological Bulletin, 138*(4), 655–691. https://doi.org/10.1037/a0027448

Bowlby, J. (1980). *Attachment and loss: Vol. 3. Loss, sadness, and depression*. Basic Books.

Bowlby, J. (1988). *A secure base: Parent-child attachment and healthy human development*. Basic Books.

Bowen, M. (1978). *Family therapy in clinical practice.* Jason Aronson.

Bradbury, T. N., & Fincham, F. D. (1990). Attributions in marriage: Review and critique. *Psychological Bulletin, 107*(1), 3–33. https://doi.org/10.1037/0033-2909.107.1.3

Canary, D. J., & Dindia, K. (2013). *Maintaining relationships through communication*. Routledge.

Carver, C. S., Scheier, M. F., & Segerstrom, S. C. (2010). Optimism. *Clinical Psychology Review, 30*(7), 879–889. https://doi.org/10.1016/j.cpr.2010.01.006

Cohen, S., & Pressman, S. D. (2006). Positive affect and health. *Current Directions in Psychological Science, 15*(3), 122–125. https://doi.org/10.1111/j.0963-7214.2006.00420.x

David, J., & Milward, T. (2013). Analyzing conflict and communication in marital relationships. *Journal of Family Communication, 13*(3), 217–235.

Dew, J. P., & Stewart, R. (2012). A financial issue, a relationship issue, or both? Examining the predictors of marital financial conflict. *Journal of Financial Therapy, 3*(1), Article 3. https://doi.org/10.4148/jft.v3i1.1455

Duck, S. (1994). *Meaningful relationships: Talking, sense, and relating*. Sage.

Edmondson, A. C. (2018). *The fearless organization: Creating psychological safety in the workplace for learning, innovation, and growth*. Wiley.

Finkel, E. J., Rusbult, C. E., Kumashiro, M., & Hannon, P. A. (2015). The suffocation of marriage: Climbing Mount Maslow without enough oxygen. *Psychological Inquiry, 26*(1), 1–41. https://doi.org/10.1080/1047840X.2015.1004994

Fitzsimons, G. M., & Bargh, J. A. (2003). Thinking of you: Nonconscious pursuit of interpersonal goals associated with relationship partners. *Journal of Personality and Social Psychology, 84*(1), 148–164. https://doi.org/10.1037/0022-3514.84.1.148

Freud, S. (1958). *Beyond the pleasure principle* (J. Strachey, Trans.). W. W. Norton. (Original work published 1920)

Garbinsky, E. N., Gladstone, J. J., Nikolova, H., & Olson, J. G. (2020). Love, lies, and money: Financial infidelity in romantic relationships. *Journal of Consumer Research, 47*(1), 1–23. https://doi.org/10.1093/jcr/ucz052

Goleman, D. (1995). *Emotional intelligence: Why it can matter more than IQ*. Bantam Books.

Gottman, J. (1994). *Why marriages succeed or fail: And how you can make yours last*. Simon & Schuster.

Gottman, J., & Silver, N. (1999). *The seven principles for making marriage work*. Crown Publishing.

Haggerty, G., et al. (2022). *The disconnected couple: Clinical perspectives on emotional distance in intimate relationships*. Routledge.

Heider, F. (1958). *The psychology of interpersonal relations*. Wiley.

Herman, J. L. (1992). *Trauma and recovery*. Basic Books.

Jackson White Law. (n.d.). *What year of a marriage is divorce most common?* https://www.jacksonwhitelaw.com

Lee, L. O., et al. (2019). Optimism and exceptional longevity: A study of older U.S. men and women.

Proceedings of the National Academy of Sciences, 116(37), 18357–18362. https://doi.org/10.1073/pnas.1900712116

Markman, H. J., Stanley, S. M., & Blumberg, S. L. (2010). *Fighting for your marriage*. Jossey-Bass.

Maslach, C., & Leiter, M. P. (2016). Burnout: A multidimensional perspective. In C. L. Cooper & I. T. Robertson (Eds.), *Professional burnout* (pp. 19–32). Psychology Press.

McNally, S., Montgomery, C., & Park, K. (2014). Marriage and family: Implications for social well-being. *Journal of Social Sciences, 6*(2), 111–120.

Mund, M., Hagemeyer, B., Benninghoven, D., & Back, M. D. (2020). Lonely me, lonely you: Associations between partner's loneliness and individual well-being. *Journal of Happiness Studies, 21*(8), 2727–2746. https://doi.org/10.1007/s10902-019-00195-8

Perry, B. D. (2009). Examining child maltreatment through a neurodevelopmental lens: Clinical applications of the neurosequential model of therapeutics. *Journal of Loss and Trauma, 14*(4), 240–255. https://doi.org/10.1080/15325020903004350

Perry, B. D., & Szalavitz, M. (2017). *The boy who was raised as a dog: And other stories from a child psychiatrist's notebook*. Basic Books.

Porges, S. W. (2011). *The polyvagal theory: Neurophysiological foundations of emotions, attachment, communication, and self-regulation*. W. W. Norton & Company.

Rogers, C. R. (1961). *On becoming a person: A therapist's view of psychotherapy*. Houghton Mifflin.

Ruus, A. (2011). Factors influencing divorce and relationship satisfaction. *Journal of Family Studies, 17*(2), 144–156.

Sullivan, H., Weber, A., & Johnson, P. (2010). The impact of divorce on children's well-being: A review of the evidence. *Journal of Child and Family Studies, 19*(3), 356–368.

Vangelisti, A. L., & Young, S. L. (2000). When words hurt: The interpersonal effects of perceived expectations and criticism. *Communication Research, 27*(1), 50–78. https://doi.org/10.1177/009365000027001003

van der Kolk, B. A. (2014). *The body keeps the score: Brain, mind, and body in the healing of trauma*. Viking.

WF Lawyers. (n.d.). *Divorce statistics and facts*. https://www.wf-lawyers.com

Made in the USA
Coppell, TX
18 February 2026

71776423R00115